THE · BUSINESS · SIDE · OF · GENERAL · PRACTICE

 Making Sense of
Fundholding

Edited by

STEPHEN HENRY

*General Practitioner, former Chairman,
National Association of Fundholding Practices*

and

DAVID PICKERSGILL

*General Practitioner, Member of the
General Medical Services Committee,
Member of the British Medical Association Council*

Foreword by

ALASDAIR LIDDELL

*Director of Planning and Performance Management,
NHS Executive*

RADCLIFFE MEDICAL PRESS
OXFORD and NEW YORK

© 1995 Stephen Henry and David Pickersgill

Radcliffe Medical Press Ltd
18 Marcham Road, Abingdon, Oxon OX14 1AA, UK

Radcliffe Medical Press, Inc
141 Fifth Avenue, New York, NY 10010, USA

British Library Cataloguing in Publication Data

A catalogue record for this book is available from the British Library.

Library of Congress Cataloging-in-Publication Data is available.

ISBN 1 85775 041 1

Typeset by Advance Typesetting Ltd, Oxfordshire
Printed and bound in Great Britain by Biddles Ltd, Guildford and King's Lynn

# ☉ Contents

# List of contributors

DAVID ARCHER, *General Practitioner; Chairman, West Midlands Association Fundholding Practices*

PAT ARCHER, *Secretary, West Midlands Association Fundholding Practices*

DAVID COLIN-THOME, *General Practitioner, Runcorn, Cheshire*

JOHN ELLIS, *Director of Fundholding, Hertfordshire Health Agency*

MALCOLM FOX, *General Practitioner, Macclesfield, Cheshire*

JENNY GRIFFITHS, *Chief Executive, Hertfordshire Health Agency*

STEPHEN HENRY, *General Practitioner, former Chairman, National Association of Fundholding Practices*

STEPHEN JONES, *Service Development Manager, Cardiff Fundholding Group*

PETER KEMP, *Director of Social Services, Durham County Council*

PAUL LAMBDEN, *Chief Executive, East Hertfordshire NHS Trust*

ALAN MAYNARD, *Professor of Economics and Director of the Centre for Health Economics, University of York*

GEOFF MEADS, *Director of Primary and Community Care, NHS Executive, South and West*

LESLEY MORRIS, *General Manager, Trowbridge, Wilts*

RHIDIAN MORRIS, *General Practitioner, Chairman, National Association of Fundholding Practices*

BERNADETTE NAUGHTON, *Business Manager, Fundholding Practice, Hon. Sec. National Association of Fundholding Practices*

CLIVE PARR, *General Manager, Hereford and Worcester Family Health Services Authority*

DAVID PICKERSGILL, *General Practitioner, Member of the General Medical Services Committee, Member of the British Medical Association Council*

TIM RICHARDSON, *General Practitioner, Epsom, Surrey*

BOB SENIOR, *Partner, Brooking Knowles & Lawrence*

WILLIE SIME, *Associate Director of Finance, Hertfordshire Health Agency*

PETER SMITH, *General Practitioner, Medical Director, Kingston and Richmond Multifund*

BILL TAYLOR, *Fundholding Adviser, BG Consulting*

JOHN WILKINSON, *Director of Finance, Hertfordshire Health Agency*

# The Business Side of General Practice

## Editorial Board for the Series

# 👓 Foreword

This book is a comprehensive introduction to GP fundholding. It offers practical guidance on the day to day realities of running a fund, and sets this in context against the policies which have underpinned the scheme. It will be of particular interest to those considering fundholding as a result of the recent announcements about the extension of the scheme; equally, there are fresh insights for the experienced observer.

The list of contributors is impressive; in their own way, all have been instrumental in the successful development of fundholding at local or national level. From Alan Maynard's provocative scene-setting to David Colin-Thome's vision of the future, this is an interesting and instructive account from fundholders, managers and academics who have been closely involved with the scheme from its inception, expressing their own views from their own very different experiences.

*Making Sense of Fundholding* is a comprehensive guide to the current scheme which has truly empowered GPs within the reformed NHS. Inevitably as the scheme develops and expands there will be changes, but the fundamental principles set out here will remain unchanged.

Alasdair Liddell
Director of Planning and
Performance Management
NHS Executive
December 1994

# Preface

The introduction of the internal market in the NHS and in particular the development of fundholding, created a huge challenge for general practitioners, hospitals and health service managers alike. The fundholding scheme itself created deep divisions within the medical profession when it was first proposed and there are still many doctors who are fiercely opposed to it. However, a very significant number of doctors are now fundholders, and four years into the scheme it seems an appropriate time to take stock of what has been achieved and how fundholding is likely to develop in the years ahead. This book, through its authors, draws on the experience of a wide range of people involved with the scheme, from within general practice itself and from various parts of the NHS management structure.

It will be of interest not only to prospective fundholders, but also to those already involved in the scheme. As time has gone by, each practice, each provider unit and each FHSA have evolved their own systems of management and organization, and there is a great deal to be learnt from studying the methods used in different parts of the country.

We are extremely grateful to the various authors for their contributions. They are all closely involved with fundholding and their knowledge and expertise should be of great interest and considerable benefit to readers of this book.

We have not set out to make any political statement about the fundholding scheme, but we hope that the book will provide a practical assessment of the scheme as it currently operates, together with useful advice and information for all those who are involved or are likely to become involved in the future. We are indebted to colleagues within the British Medical Association and the National Association of Fundholding Practices who have given us much useful advice and encouragement in the preparation of this book.

Stephen Henry
David Pickersgill
December 1994

# New Fundholding Management Allowances

As this book went to press in December 1994, the new fundholding management allowances were announced.

Readers should note that the management allowance which is referred to in the text as being set at £35 000 per annum per practice, is to be changed in April 1995. A scale of allowances will then be payable as follows:

- a basic allowance of £27 258 for each 'standard fundholding' practice

- a supplement based on list size of:
  - 0–6999 patients at £1.88 per patient
  - 7000–10 999, £1.61 per patient
  - 11 000–14 999, £1.52 per patient
  - 15 000–20 999, £1.17 per patient
  - 21 000 plus, £1.02 per patient

- a group allowance of £1400 for each practice in excess of one in the fundholding scheme

- a site allowance of £650 for each major branch surgery

- in the preparatory year:
  - a basic allowance of £21 255
  - a group allowance of £2800
  - a site allowance of £650

- community GP fundholders will get:
  - an allowance, irrespective of list size, of £14 135
  - a group allowance of £1250
  - a site allowance of £650

- in the preparatory year:
  - a flat allowance of £8312
  - a group allowance of £2500
  - a site allowance of £650
  - a shift allowance of £13 123 for community fundholding practices wishing to prepare for standard GP fundholding.

# 1  Whither Fundholding?

## Alan Maynard

## Introduction

In June 1984, the Office of Health Economics (OHE) organized a conference at Cumberland Lodge in Windsor Great Park to address 'solutions' to the then current NHS crisis. John Vaisey, an economist and a politician who started life as an adviser to Harold Wilson and by then was a Conservative member of the House of Lords, argued that the only solution to the problems of the NHS was to change its financial basis and fund it by private insurance.

My response to this proposal was to argue that multiple funding sources usually led to cost inflation (as evidenced by the experience in the USA) and that private insurers were equal to the NHS in their ineffectiveness in using their purchasing power to control provider behaviour and ensure that health care was delivered cost-effectively. To mitigate inefficiency in the use of scarce NHS resources it was, I argued, necessary to reform the provider not the finance side of the NHS.

Provider reform should, in principle, be built around the idea of giving groups of GPs budgets with which they could buy diagnostic and therapeutic hospital services and other care packages. Thus began what is now known as GP fundholding (GPFH).

This notion was reported in the conference proceedings by Marshall Marinker[1]. In this and subsequent publications[2,3] it was argued that the notion of the GP as fundholder should be the subject of a carefully designed and evaluated pilot experiment which, if successful, should be used to guide national policy.

One of the political participants at the original OHE conference at Cumberland Lodge was David Willetts, now Conservative MP for Havant. The combined effect of the advocacy of academics such as Marinker and Maynard and the work of David Willetts (who at that time was Director of the Centre for Policy Studies, the Conservative

Think Tank), was that the notion of GPFH was quite well developed by the end of the 1980s when it fell on the ears of a Secretary of State who was desperately seeking radical reform.

The inclusion of GPFH in the 1989 White Paper *Working for Patients* created what has been described as both a maverick and a catalyst. What are its strengths and weaknesses? How should it be developed?

Before the GPFH experiment can be appraised and the options for its development evaluated, the goals of the NHS must be identified and the difficulty of achieving these goals examined.

# The performance of the NHS

Usually policy makers internationally place differing degrees of emphasis on three goals: equity, efficiency and cost containment.

## Equity

The equity goal relates to equalizing access to health care by minimizing price and time costs and redistributing resources by budget formulae (such as Resource Allocation Working Party [RAWP]) to equalize the financial capacity of different geographical areas to provide health care. In general the NHS has been quite successful in equalizing access to health care although substantial inequalities remain in health and health care as demonstrated by, for instance, the Black Report[4]. The inequalities that remain in primary care are the products of the Government's failure 'to RAWP' the general medical service budget, which, if implemented, would generate major shifts in resources and personnel from the well-endowed South of England to the deprived North[5].

The equalization of health chances requires more than the redistribution of NHS resources. Health inequalities are the product of inequalities in endowments (genetic, income, wealth, education and housing) and behaviours (i.e. social class differences in for example exercise, diet, work environments, and use of addictive substances (especially tobacco)). Compensating variations in health care can make little contribution to reducing inequalities in health because of the unproven cost-effectiveness of most interventions and the difficulties associated with targeting NHS resources on those whose capacity to benefit may be less than the more affluent, middle class and voter-active.

## Cost containment

The NHS has been relatively successful in containing cost inflation. The British spend about 6% of their Gross Domestic Product (GDP) on health care. People in the USA spend over 14½% of a much larger GDP on health care but do not live very much longer or have better quality lives. The NHS, with one primary funder, is much more conservative in its use of resources, and funding has grown slowly (as shown by the data in Table 1.1: over the period the share of the General Medical Services (GMS) was quite stable, at about 21% of the total). This cost control has been most effective for the hospital and social services budgets, which are cash limited. The primary care budget, which is demand determined, has grown more rapidly and is much more difficult to constrain.

## Efficiency

No health-care system is efficient because most interventions, diagnostic and therapeutic, are unproven – i.e. there is no knowledge base, derived from good clinical trials. Many patients who present to GPs are ill but due to unknown causes! Hospital consultants confronted by patients of similar age, sex and condition provide treatments which differ considerably, e.g. small area variations in chemotherapy have been shown to exceed eight-fold in some health-care markets. This variation is unsurprising: it is the product of ignorance about the cost-effectiveness of alternative therapies and uncertainty about the appropriate treatment.

The issue of inefficiency is the major problem confronting policy makers and practioners in all health-care systems. It is essential both to identify 'what works' and to determine the cost-effective means of teaching old (and not so old) docs new tricks!

Where there is knowledge of effectiveness, it is often ignored. For instance, there is trial evidence to support the prophylactic use of antibiotics for caesarian sections; there is evidence that many diagnostic D&C procedures are useless, expensive and risky; and there is evidence that 'watchful waiting' is the appropriate response for young children with 'glue ear'. This evidence is ignored by many practitioners.

In primary care service development has been rapid but unevaluated. There has, for instance, been a rapid increase in the use of practice nurses and nurse practitioners. The skill mix in primary care has changed but is largely unevaluated[6]. Evaluation is always difficult and costly but may prove less expensive than unevaluated developments driven by rhetoric and good intentions.

Table 1.1 UK National Health and personal social service gross expenditure 1978–79 to 1992–93 (£ billion)

| Year | Total expenditure | Annual percentage increase | Real expenditure (1991–92 prices)[a] | Annual percentage increase | Volume expenditure (1990–91 prices)[b] | Annual percentage increase |
|---|---|---|---|---|---|---|
| 1978–79 | 9.2 | – | 24.9 | – | 30.7 | – |
| 1979–80 | 11.1 | 20.7 | 25.7 | 3.3 | 30.7 | 0.1 |
| 1980–81 | 14.1 | 27.0 | 27.6 | 7.4 | 30.5 | –0.8 |
| 1981–82 | 15.8 | 12.1 | 28.2 | 2.3 | 31.6 | 3.6 |
| 1982–83 | 17.2 | 8.9 | 28.7 | 1.6 | 32.3 | 2.2 |
| 1983–84 | 18.3 | 6.4 | 29.1 | 1.7 | 32.7 | 1.2 |
| 1984–85 | 19.6 | 7.1 | 29.7 | 1.9 | 33.1 | 1.2 |
| 1985–86 | 20.7 | 5.6 | 29.7 | 0.1 | 33.2 | 0.4 |
| 1986–87 | 22.3 | 7.7 | 31.1 | 4.4 | 33.4 | 0.8 |
| 1987–88 | 24.5 | 9.9 | 32.3 | 4.1 | 33.9 | 1.3 |
| 1988–89 | 27.0 | 10.2 | 33.2 | 2.7 | 33.8 | –0.3 |
| 1989–90 | 29.5 | 9.3 | 34.1 | 2.6 | 34.5 | 2.0 |
| 1990–91 | 33.1 | 12.2 | 35.4 | 3.9 | 36.0 | 4.5 |
| 1991–92 | 37.4 | 13.0 | 37.4 | 5.6 | 37.4 | 3.9 |
| 1992–93 | 41.0 | 9.6 | 39.3 | 5.1 | – | – |
| Overall percentage change 1978–79 to 1991–92 | 305 | | 50.4 | | 21.96 | |

[a] Cash figures adjusted to 1991–92 price levels using the GDP deflator.
[b] Cash figures adjusted to 1991–92 price levels using the Hospital and Community Health Services Pay and Prices deflator.

Source: Public Expenditure Analyses to 1995–96, Treasury, 1993.

Thus the goals of the NHS are difficult to achieve. Whilst cost containment has been achieved for the hospital budget and local authority social services owing to cash limits, the primary-care budget is open-ended and more difficult to constrain. Whilst the NHS has performed well in equity terms, the primary-care budget is distributed unevenly. It, like all other health-care systems, operates in a knowledge vacuum about cost-effectiveness and uses scarce health-care resources inefficiently.

# An evaluation of general practice fundholding

Those who developed the principles of GPFH in the 1980s hoped for its careful evaluation in a properly designed trial. Political expediency prohibited such evaluation as Kenneth Clarke (then Secretary of State) believed it would delay the reform process. Hence GPFH was introduced cumulatively, and by 1994 more than one in three GPs were working in fundholding practices.

The evaluation of this major development has been inadequate. Glennerster et al.[7,8] have produced qualitative studies of succeeding waves of fundholders. These studies are based on small numbers and limited statistical analysis. Coulter and her colleagues[9] have evaluated the activities of some GPFHs around Oxford. Inter alia, she found that their prescribing costs appear to be lower, but like other behaviours of GPFHs this may be due to the characteristics of the practices (highly motivated, well organized) and their patients (mostly (70%) middle class) rather than the performance of fundholders.

The National Audit Office has collected data from 105 GPFHs and 105 non-GPFHs. This study will be published in the summer of 1994 and will be followed up with further work by the Audit Commission in 1994–95.

Thus the empirical basis on which to judge fundholding is, as yet, very limited. Questions such as what criteria, if any, were used by Regions in the selection of applicants for GP fundholding status remain unanswered. Were all and any applicants accepted by Regions for GPFH status? If so, whilst this might have been appropriate for the initial first wave, is it appropriate for the maybe less well qualified subsequent waves?

What criteria were used to determine the funding of GPFHs? Historic costs (plus?) appear to be an answer to this question; but what historic periods were used, and if the budgets were cost plus how was the 'plus' determined? How will future budgets be determined? HM Treasury is concerned about the cost of GPFH and the intention set out by Government since 1989 has been to move to capitation-based funding. Unfortunately, given practices' small population size, the basis of needs-related capitation funding is difficult to determine as appropriate statistics are not collected routinely.

What surpluses have evolved each year? How do these surpluses vary and for what purposes have they been spent? How carefully have Regions monitored the accounts of GPFHs and ensured that their expenditures have been consistent with the 'rules of the game'?

It is questions such as these, concerned with how the processes of developing GPFH have been conducted, as well as the costs, activities and outcomes of the new organizations themselves, which must be addressed. The most significant apparent benefit of fundholding appears to be the empowerment of GPs. The power relationships have been reversed in many areas: the usual joke is that GPFHs no longer send Christmas cards to hospital consultants to get their patients preferential treatment but they get them from hospital consultants anxious to ensure continuity of contracts and income from GPFHs. The creation of this power has, it is argued, given many GPFHs the confidence to manage their external and internal relationships more vigorously and improve the quality of the service they offer their patients.

However, overall the benefits of fundholding are poorly described and inadequately evaluated. Furthermore it is impossible to compare these benefits with the significant costs of this innovatory policy. For a pioneer of the GP funding idea this is deeply frustrating.

## Whither general practice fundholding?

Major changes are likely in both the provision of primary care and GPFH. The 1990 GP contract was badly designed[10] and increased management costs in general practice. This contract was the product of politicians discovering that professional ethics had been an inadequate control on the delivery of primary care. By the late 1980s the politicians had realized that they did not know what services GPs delivered, let alone whether they were cost-effective. Furthermore, as elsewhere in all health-care systems, there were large unexplained variations in GP activity (e.g. referral patterns and pharmaceutical prescribing) with some less active GPs apparently consuming significant levels of 'on the job leisure'!

GPFH consortia are emerging in significant numbers and investing in specialized management services. Such groups are 'shopping around' and developing their purchaser powers in innovative and effective ways. Some groups of non-GP fundholders are also emerging, particpating in locality planning and collaborating with DHA purchasers. Such GP-led purchasing consortia, if successful, may absorb and replace District purchasers if policy makers in the reformed NHS, which is more highly centralized than it was before the reforms, allow flexibility and innovation.

Such large primary care-led purchasing consortia could develop both services and skill mix in radical ways. This innovation may be fuelled by changes in the GP remuneration system. If 24-hour cover is removed as an element in the GP contract as is being currently discussed, new ways of remunerating GPs will emerge (e.g. salary) and the ways in which patient cover is provided will have to change radically.

In city centres primary care 'shops' will probably emerge, sometimes located in hospitals. Some London accident and emergency centres are already nurse based, and primary care 'shops' will probably increasingly be dominated by nurses and nurse practitioners supervised by GPs.

Such change may be led by private firms who might contract to provide primary care and other services with Family Health Services Authorities (FHSAs). At present the FHSA–GP contract is an agency–individual-practioner arrangement. However, in future FHSAs may go out to tender and ask for competitive bids from groups of GPs and private groups, both types of bidder offering radical provision arrangements which exploit substitution possibilities between the skilled and unskilled (e.g. nurse practitioner or nurse assistants) and between skill types (e.g. doctors or nurses or counsellors). Such arrangements could exploit underused skills to manage elements of the contract more cost-effectively (e.g. pharmacists could be given the right to alter GPs' prescriptions if generics were specifically indicated).

Such innovation requires Government willingness to be flexible, avoiding narrow regulation and encouraging innovation. This attitude may be encouraged by constraints on public expenditure and an ideological preference to privatize the provision of health care. If the system changes in this manner, change must be evaluated although such behaviour will probably once again not be 'politically opportune'!

## Conclusions

Fundholding by GPs means that they control finance and purchase health care on behalf of their patients. The weakest element in the NHS reforms is the purchasing function, in part because it is dominated by consultants in public health medicine who seem more intent on inventing 'needs' rather than focusing on where the best care at the lowest price is available. With GPs, both fundholders and non-fundholders, forming coalitions, these primary-care coalitions are covering 200 000 to 300 000 people, populations similar to DHAs.

The scope for strategic behaviour (i.e. cost shifting) between GPFHs and DHA purchasers is significant and it may be efficient for the former to take over the latter. Indeed, competing GPFH coalitions could offer some patients choice of purchaser in urban areas.

At present Government strategy on fundholding and many of the other issues discussed in this chapter seems at best tentative, at worst confused and inconsistent. The scope for stifling innovation seems to be considerable and the momentum of change produced by fundholding may be removed by Whitehall panic about its cost and the failure of policy makers, researchers and practitioners to evaluate change and 'confuse' public choices with facts. The price of producing such knowledge may be high but the cost of inadequate evaluation may be greater and create the opportunity for a bold experiment to be murdered in its childhood! Such homicidal tendencies may be reinforced by defensive (quiet life) contracting by fundholders. In the medium term, the survival of GPFH will only be possible if it is demonstrated to be innovative and cost-effective.

# References

1   Marinker M (1984) Developments in primary care. In G. Teeling Smith (ed). *A New NHS Act for 1996?* Office of Health Economics, London.

2   Maynard A (1986) Performance incentives. In G. Teeling Smith (ed). *Health Education and General Practice*. Office of Health Economics, London.

3   Maynard A, Marinker M and Pereira Gray D (1986) The doctor, the patient and their contract: III Alternative contracts are viable? *British Medical Journal* 292: 1438–40.

4   Townsend P and Davidson N (1982) *Inequalities in Health – The Black Report*. Penguin, London.

5   Birch S and Maynard A (1986) *RAWPing the NHS Budgets*. Discussion Paper 19, Centre for Health Economics, University of York.

6   Heath I (1994) Skill mix in primary care. *British Medical Journal* **308**: 993–4.

7   Glennerster H, Matsaganis M and Owens P (1992) *A Foothold for Fund-holding*. King's Fund, London.

8   Glennerster H, Matsaganis M, Owens P and Hancock S (1994) GP Fund-holding: wild card or winning hand? In R. Robinson and J. Le Grand (eds). *Evaluating the NHS Reforms*. King's Fund, London.

9   Coulter A, Klassen A, MacKensie IZ and McPherson K (1993) Diagnostic dilation and curettage: Is it used appropriately? *British Medical Journal* **306**: 236–9.

10  Scott T and Maynard A (1991) *Will the New GP Contract Lead to Cost Effective Medical Practice?* Discussion Paper 82, Centre for Health Economics, University of York.

# 2   The Regulations

## David Pickersgill

Fundholding, like all other parts of a GP's NHS activities, is governed by NHS Regulations. These were originally published in 1990 as Statutory Instrument No. 1753, subsequently amended in 1991 by Statutory Instrument No. 582 and again in April 1993 by Statutory Instrument No. 567. Following the Secretary of State's announcement about changes to the Fundholding Scheme at the Conservative Party Conference in Autumn 1994, further new amendments to be introduced in 1996 will provide for three tiers of fundholding; with the minimum list being 5000 patients for standard fundholding and a list of 3000 for the new concept of 'community fundholding'. This will enable practices to hold a budget for staff, drugs, diagnostic tests and community services. Mercifully, they are considerably shorter than the Regulations which cover our provision of general medical services (GMS) and are considerably easier to read and understand.

The first set of Regulations relate to the application for recognition of a fundholding practice, the granting of such recognition and the conditions for continuing recognition. They cover the failure of an RHA to approve an application, appeals against such decisions and the consequences of removal of fundholding status. The final part of the Regulations covers the 'allotted sum' and the authorized purposes for which it can be used, including payment for drugs, medicines and listed appliances, payments for goods and services and payment of salaries.

The 1991 amendments were relatively minor and related primarily to doctors practising on the borders of England and Scotland who had patients in both countries. Thankfully the Regulations were re-issued in full and published as a single document. A further Statutory Instrument in 1993 included several additional amendments and expanded on the earlier Regulations, including new provisions relating to the supply of goods and services by fundholding practices themselves and provision for the recovery of 'misapplied amounts'. Regulations to allow the purchase of nursing and certain other community services were also introduced.

## Applying for recognition as a fundholding practice

Regulation 3 requires an application to be lodged with the RHA by 1 April in the year prior to that for which fundholding status is being sought for the first time. The application must be signed by all members of the partnership, and the practice is required to provide any information and documents which the RHA may reasonably require to determine the application. The conditions for obtaining recognition as a fundholding practice are spelt out as Schedule 1 to the 1993 Regulations and specify that there must be at least 7000 patients on the list of the practice, or that the practice list size will be 7000 by the date on which fundholding commences. In the case of applications by two or more practices, none of the partners must be in a practice whose list size is already 7000. Legislation to be introduced in 1995 will enable practices with list sizes of only 3000 patients to apply for 'community fundhold-ing'. This fund will cover community services, diagnostic tests, staff and prescribing costs. The list size requirement for standard fundholding will be 5000. The RHA is required to satisfy itself that the practice will be capable of managing the fund effectively and efficiently and has adequate staff and computer facilities to enable it to do this. The members of the practice or practices also have to agree to comply with the conditions for continuing recognition as a fundholding practice, and where they are not members of a single partnership they have to sign an agreement approved by the RHA which effectively makes them jointly and severally liable for any act by a member of the practices in relation to the fund.

Given the complex nature of managing a fund, any practice making an application must be absolutely sure that all the members of the partner-ship are happy about the application and that they are all satisfied that both they and their staff are capable of managing the fund and the computer systems necessary to administer it. Because of the financial implications of individual partner's actions it is vitally important that partnerships are able to agree joint policies in relation to prescribing, referral patterns, employment of staff, etc. This is even more important when more than one practice is submitting a joint application.

Family Health Services Authorities (FHSAs) have been encouraged to identify practices eligible and interested in becoming fundholders, and they will send application forms to the practice several months in advance of the application date. They will require details of the practice's management arrangements, prescribing policies, computer systems and a short statement outlining its reasons for wishing to join the fundholding scheme. This will be followed up by an FHSA visit to the practice, and the FHSA will then forward the application and their observations on the practice's ability to manage a fund to the RHA. RHAs will determine applications usually by the end of February, giving the practice one month before they enter the preparatory year. At this stage the practice must decide whether to commit itself to the fundholding scheme and complete a formal application. This is usually accompanied by a statement as to how they plan to spend the management allowance and is followed up by a detailed data collection and assessment over the next few months to allow the preliminary budget to be set towards the end of the calendar year prior to fundholding actually commencing. Also during the autumn of that year practices must send their FHSA a purchasing plan which will include at least a statement of how they satisfy the assessment criteria and information about the types of contract which they intend to place and the provider units which they intend to use. All of this information will be assessed and final approval as a fundholding practice should be granted by the end of February, one month before fundholding actually begins. This approval will usually be accompanied by the firm budget offer.

Where an RHA has refused a practice approval to become fundholding there is a right of appeal. No time limit is imposed on this appeal, and an appeal does not need to be signed by all members of the partnership.

## Applying to become a fundholder: Summary

1 *September and October each year*: FHSAs identify practices eligible to become fundholders 18 or 19 months later. Practices receive eligibility criteria and application forms.

2 *Before end of January*: FHSA undertakes practice visits and makes recommendations to RHA concerning suitability of practices to commence preparatory year.

3 *Before end of February*: RHA grants approval to those practices it considers suitable to commence preparatory work.

4 *By mid-March*: Details of spending intentions for preparatory allowance to be sent to the FHSA.

5 *By end of March*: Application form for recognition as a fundholding practice to be completed and received by FHSA. This must be signed by all the partners in the practice.

6 *April to September* of preparatory year data collection takes place. This will include information from discharge letters received by the practice together with numbers of diagnostic tests and requests for referrals which the GPs have made during that time.

7 *By December 31*: Practices submit to FHSA a purchasing plan, including a statement of how they propose to place contracts, satisfy the assessment criteria and plan to use the management allowance.

8 *End of February*: Successful applicants will be informed that they may become fundholders and will receive the fund offer at that time.

9 *End of March*: Agreement must have been reached with the RHA on the level of funding not later than one month after the offer was made.

## Continued recognition as a fundholding practice

A further schedule (2) to the Regulations contains details of the criteria practices must fulfil to continue as fundholders. The list size criteria must be fulfilled and the need to have an agreement between the partners of differing partnerships must also be met exactly as in the criteria for the original application. The RHA must satisfy itself that the practice has administered the fund efficiently and effectively during the previous year and that no part of the fund has been used for any purpose other than those specified in the Regulations. If a fundholding practice employs a person to provide any services directly to patients, that employee must be appropriately qualified and have the training and experience deemed necessary by the RHA to provide those services.

The practice must also maintain a fundholding bank account for the purpose of receiving any payments from the fund, specifically those relating to practice staff, payment for any services directly provided and payment to the practice of any savings which have been accrued in earlier years. Further criteria require the practice to have provided the FHSA with various reports during the preceding year and annual accounts must have been submitted to the FHSA within 6 weeks of the end of the financial year to which the accounts relate. Given the delays in obtaining invoices from provider units and the difficulties of using some computer software programs this is an extremely difficult criterion to fulfil, and fundholding practices may find themselves submitting year end accounts which contain several estimated payments and provisional balance sheets. A sound knowledge of basic accounting is an essential requirement for fund managers, as is ready access to professional accountancy advice. Finally, there are strict criteria to be met in relation to any payments received by the practice for services provided directly to patients. The 1993 Amendments to the Regulations precluded the use of Limited Companies for the provision of such services and specified a very restrictive list of services which practices can provide directly and for which they may be reimbursed.

The Regulations contain details of the appeals mechanism and also information relating to the appointment of additional partners, or the withdrawal of partners from a fundholding practice.

## Renunciation of recognition

If a majority of partners in a practice notify the RHA that they intend to renounce their fundholding status they must do so at least one month before the 31 March following the sending of the notice. They must submit details of any NHS contracts into which the practice has entered, the amount remaining in the fundholding account and details of any savings which have been accrued from the fund. They must also supply details of the liabilities of any members of the fundholding practice. They must continue to fulfil their obligations as fundholders until the RHA has satisfied itself that all the liabilities of their former fundholding status have been discharged.

## Removal of recognition of fundholding status

As well as practices being able to withdraw voluntarily, RHAs may decide to remove fundholding status from a practice. The Regulations contain details of how this can be done and lay down a specific procedure. There are arrangements for practices to make oral representations to the RHA and for them to appeal formally against such a decision to the Secretary of State. Provision is also made for the anticipated rare circumstance where immediate removal of fundholding recognition may be required. The Regulations provide only two circumstances in which this can happen, namely that it is:

- in the interests of patients of members of the practice or

- for the purpose of ensuring the proper management of the allotted sum.

## 'Allotted sum authorized purposes'

The fund covers:
- hospital services
- community health services
- drugs
- practice staff.

There is considerable detail in the Regulations about the amount which will be paid for drugs, medicines and listed appliances. This sum is normally agreed by the practice with the FHSA Prescribing Adviser towards the end of the year preceding that to which the fund relates. The various goods and services which can be paid for from the fund are also specified and are broadly described as the purchase of such goods and services other than GMS which are referred to in the Regulations and as are considered necessary for the proper treatment of individuals on the lists of patients of the members of the practice.

The fund excludes:
- emergency treatment
- obstetrics
- genito-urinary medicine
- inpatient stays which do not include a listed operation or procedure.

The 1993 Regulations also included provision for the purchase of district nursing and health visiting services and go on to spell out the circumstances in which a fundholding practice may purchase goods or services from a member of the practice or someone who is connected with a member of the practice, making it quite clear that the RHA must approve any such arrangements.

## Payment of salaries

As one might expect, the use of part of the fund for the payment of practice staff is governed by the Regulations. In addition to spelling out who can be reimbursed under these arrangements they also make clear that this part of the fund cannot be used for employing or engaging the services of an additional doctor to provide GMS. An additional doctor can be employed to provide the special list of services which fundholders can supply outside the GMS provisions.

## Savings

The use of savings which fundholders may have achieved has been one of the most hotly debated aspects of the whole fundholding scheme. There is a popular misconception amongst many non-fundholders that fundholding GPs can somehow benefit directly from the use of such savings. The Regulations spell out the following purposes to which such savings can be put.

- The purchase of material or equipment which

  - can be used for the treatment of patients of the practice
  - enhances the comfort or convenience of patients of the practice
  - enables the practice to be managed more effectively and efficiently.

- The purchase of material or equipment relating to health education.

- The improvement of any premises from which the members of the practice carry on their practice, whether by improving the structure of the premises or the purchase of   furniture and furnishings for the premises.

This makes it absolutely clear that no fundholding GP can benefit directly from any savings which the practice may have made as a result of its fundholding activities, although one might argue that if the premises were substantially improved and increased in value, or if equipment was purchased which had a residual value at the time of a partner's retirement, then his or her share of the practice assets may be increased and the partner may take out of the practice a larger sum of money than that which he or she would have been able to do had the practice not provided its improved premises or additional equipment from this source.

In general, practices who have managed to achieve savings would be well advised to think very carefully about which part of the fund they have managed to make savings from and how they intend to spend those savings, bearing in mind the high degree of suspicion amongst non-fundholders about these activities.

## Recovery of misapplied sums

The amendment Regulations which brought these paragraphs into force caused the General Medical Services Committee (GMSC) considerable anxiety. However, legal advice was obtained about the precise nature of misapplied funds. They do not relate to accidental overspends resulting, for example, from admission rates being faster than those that had been anticipated; or to the purchase of more goods and services than could be provided for from an allotted sum. They do, however, apply to the purchase of and payment for any services which a fundholding practice may make which are not covered under the fundholding Regulations. Although a practice may not find itself in contravention of this particular part of the Regulations in the case of the overspends previously referred to in this paragraph, it would of course put itself in jeopardy of failure to be granted continuing recognition as a fundholding practice if the RHA felt that it was incapable of managing its resources effectively. It is worth noting that in the event of funds being misapplied the recovery will be from the practice and not from the fund. The debt will be treated as a debt of the practice to the RHA.

## Community nursing and health visiting

The 1993 Regulations provide that fundholders' contracts with community nursing and health visiting services are:

- subject to RHA agreement

- placed with an established NHS Community Nursing Provider

- for at least the same level of service for which the practice has been funded.

There is, however, nothing to stop a practice contracting for a level of community nursing and health visiting services greater than that which is currently available.

Community health services covered by the fund:

- district nursing
- health visiting
- chiropody
- dietetics
- all community and out-patient mental health services
- mental health counselling
- health services for people with a learning disability.

## Total Purchasing

New regulations will be introduced in 1995 to enable approximately thirty pilot schemes to go ahead with so-called total purchasing. It is anticipated that this will enable GPs to purchase all hospital and community services which they use.

## Conclusion

Although the Regulations are not unduly complex, it is vitally important that every member of a fundholding practice fully understands them. Fundholding is the only activity undertaken by GPs where they have to be directly accountable for the precise sums of money that they spend. They must take great care to ensure that they do not inadvertently find themselves 'misapplying the fund' or failing to secure an appropriate level of goods and services for their patients through their contracting arrangements. Fundholders are particularly vulnerable in these areas, and a clear understanding of the Regulations is absolutely vital.

## Department Circulars and Regulations

### Circulars

Funding General Practice (December 1989).
Manual of Accounts (September 1990).
General Practice Funding (October 1990).

A Guide to the GP Funding Accounts System (October 1990).

Guidance on the Scope of the Hospital Element (November 1990).

Guidance on Contracting by Fundholders (February 1991).

General Practice Funding: Financial Matters (EL(91)36 March 1991).

List of Goods and Services Covered by the GP Fundholding Scheme (Reg 17.2 March 1991).

Joint Guidance to Hospital Consultants on GP Fundholding (EL(91)84) June 1991).

Accountability of GP Fundholders (June 1991).

End of Year Guidance for GP Fundholding Scheme (includes FDL(91)152 February 1992).

GP Practice Funding: Draft Guidance on Fundholders Purchasing and Selling Services.

Priorities and Planning Guidance 1993–4 (EL(92)47 July 1992).

Guidance on the Extension of the Hospital and Community Health Services Element of the GP Fundholding Scheme from 1 April 1993 (EL(92)48 July 1992).

Developments of Primary and Community Care – Support for Commissioning of Nursing Services, Value for Money Units Study, the District Nursing Grade Mix (EL(92)69 October 1992).

Health Services for People with Learning Disabilities (HSG(92)42).

Extension of the Hospital and Community Health Services Elements of the GP Fundholding Scheme from April 1, 1993 (HSG(92)153).

GP Fundholding Consortia (EL(92)92).

GP Fundholding Practices: the Provision of Secondary Care (HSG(93)14).

Developing NHS Purchasing and GP Fundholding (EL(94)79).

# Regulations

The National Health Service (Fundholding Practices) (Applications and Recognition) Regulations 1990 (Statutory Instrument No. 1753).

The National Health Service (Fundholding Practices) (General) Regulations 1991 (Statutory Instrument No. 582).

The National Health Service (Fundholding Practices) (Amendments) Regulations 1992 (Statutory Instrument No. 636).

HSG(93)21 Consolidates and amends the above regulations.

# 3 The Preparatory Year

## *Bernadette Naughton*

*'Plans are nothing; planning is everything'*
                                    *Dwight D Eisenhower*

By the end of the preparatory year, a practice will almost certainly be operating in a more business-like way and have taken a major step forward in planning the future provision of primary and secondary health care for its practice population.

## Application

Once a practice has taken the decision to join or even find out more about the fundholding scheme it should get in touch with its Family Health Services Authority (FHSA) or the Health Commission if the FHSA has been amalgamated. Each FHSA has a fundholding manager who is the prime source of information about the scheme and usually a key support agent during this period. The initial contact can be verbal but ideally should be made in writing.

The FHSA fundholding manager will generally wish to visit the practice and meet the GP partners and manager. The purpose of this meeting is two-fold.

- To explain the scheme and the process that will be required in the preparatory year.

- To review the practice generally (though this is subject to regional variation).

The manager will wish to be assured of the following:

- all the GP partners and manager are committed to joining the scheme
- the practice is computerized
- the practice is well managed and has a manager in post
- the practice keeps proper practice accounts.

A formal application by the practice will be required, and the FHSA fundholding manager will give advice as to the information which should be included or supply the application form, whichever is applicable.

## Appeals

If for some reason the practice application is turned down by the FHSA, the practice can then appeal to the RHA and ultimately to the Secretary of State for Health.

## Action planning

A simple but useful way of managing change is to set out each stage as a series of actions which need to be achieved (Box 3.1).

---

**Box 3.1**

Stage 1:   Application action plan – Achieved by:

1 Practice makes a decision to apply to join the fundholding scheme.
2 Practice makes contact with FHSA fundholding manager.
3 FHSA visits practice and carries out assessment.
4 Practice submits formal application.
5 FHSA informs practice of its decision.
6 If practice is turned down appeal lodged.
7 Practice accepted officially.

---

# Data collection

If the practice is to develop and progress during the preparatory year then it must achieve accurate data collection. Not renowned as one of the most exciting fundholding activities, it does however add enormous value to the process if it is set about in a logical way right from the start. Responsibility is a key word in fundholding, and no aspect of the work needs it more than data collection. The member of staff responsible for data collection should enjoy process work and be capable of operating independently.

The FHSA or Health Commission will set out their standards, but most require a practice to complete a number of returns. Many FHSAs are still using the pink GP Referral Data Collection Form which has a total of 20 sections to be completed (Figure 3.1). The practice will be expected to complete one of these forms for each patient referral for an out-patients, direct access or in-patient appointment. The collection period is usually 26 weeks from 1 April to 30 September, and the FHSA manager will advise how best to carry out the data collection exercise. The reasons for collecting data on patient referrals are:

- to count the number of referrals made to each provider unit
- to validate the data with the practice and provider unit
- to identify and iron out any problems of coding, classification, etc
- to assist with the construction of the practice budget.

The importance of accurate and comprehensive data collection cannot be overstated, as it may affect the budget for years to come.

The practice that wishes to build up a good in-house database could best achieve this by using a spreadsheet. These are cheap and capable of processing complex and volume data. Data will need to be collected on the following:

- all out-patient referrals
- all in-patient and day cases
- domiciliary visits
- diagnostic services, pathology tests and X-rays
- community nursing (health visitors, district nurses and community practice nurses)

Patient

5 Surname _____  6 Forename _____   5 and 6 Leave blank or
detach before submission

NWTRHA

| GP referral data collection form | Form Number* ☐☐☐☐ |

*Denotes Mandatory                                    **PRACTICE DETAILS**

1 Practice Address            2* Practice Code   ☐☐☐☐☐☐

☐☐☐☐☐☐☐☐☐☐☐☐☐☐☐☐☐☐☐

3* Referring GP
{PPA code - include      ☐☐☐☐☐☐
locums and assistants}

(Postcode)                   4  Responsible GP
☐☐☐☐☐☐☐                    {PPA code if different   ☐☐☐☐☐☐
from above}

7  Address                                          **PATIENT DETAILS**
Only when postcode not known

No House Numbers       8   NHS Number  _____

9*  Date of birth        ☐☐☐☐☐ 1 ☐☐☐
(DD MM CC YY)

10* Sex                  ☐
(M) ale OR (F) emale

(Postcode)*              11* Temporary Resident   ☐
☐☐☐☐☐☐☐                    Enter (Y) es OR (N) o

12* Date of referral                                **REFERRAL DETAILS**
☐☐☐☐ 1 9 9 ☐

13* Private referral         17* Referral type              ☐
Enter (Y) es OR (N) o  ☐      Enter 1-Admission 2-Outpatient
3- Direct access 4-Domiciliary

14* Hospital of referral
Enter code in box OR text below   18  Referral category        ☐
☐☐☐☐☐                          Enter 1-Advice 2-Condition Mgmt
3- Advice and condition Mgmt

15* Specialty                19  Patients condition      ☐☐☐
Enter code OR text below       Enter code in box OR text below
☐☐☐                          _____

_____

16   Consultant      20   Direct access referral    Occupational Therapy ☐

Enter (Y) es if yes  Physiotherapy ☐    Speech Therapy ☐

**Figure 3.1** GP Referral Data Collection form

- direct access services – physiotherapy, occupational therapy, speech therapy and chiropody
- child and family psychiatry.

The practice should have some mechanism in place for checking the quality of the data collected and the way it is being stored (Box 3.2). Even during the collection period of the preparatory year the practice should get into the routine of circulating the data to the doctors and other professionals who incurred the referral. In that way they will become part of the planning cycle or audit which will also soon be required.

---

**Box 3.2**

Action plan – Acknowledge the crucial importance of this exercise:

- Identify a member of staff who will be responsible for carrying out this activity.
- Be advised by your FHSA Manager as to how the data are to be collected.
- Start accurate collection for 26 weeks.
- Review in-house data requirements.
- Know what data you are expected to collect.
- Put in place a practice monitoring mechanism.

---

## Practice personnel and organization

The average GP practice has come a long way in the past few years, and fundholding usually means moving it further along the way and at a faster pace. In addition, it shifts the emphasis from the individual doctor to the practice or corporate level. The fundholding application and the budget acceptance are signed by all the partners.

Preparation of the people in the practice is, therefore, a key element of the planning. There are three levels of preparation to be considered:

- the organizational structure
- the doctors, nurses and staff
- the project or implementation group.

## The organizational structure

This is best approached by first identifying and anticipating what functions have to be performed and how roles are to be defined. Modern management theory advocates a flat organizational structure with the fewer chains of command the better, as each link in the chain represents a potential weakness. The average fundholding practice will need the following functions to operate effectively.

- Clinical, including primary and secondary care.

- Operational, including patient through-put, buildings, etc.

- Personnel, including recruitment and training.

- Financial, including items of service and practice accounts.

- Fund management, including negotiations, contracting, monitoring of all the budgets.

- Marketing, which includes managing complaints, communications and patient participation.

- Planning, which includes service and capital development.

As the practice moves further towards corporate and board level, there is a need for a supporting organizational structure. Options which support board structure are:

- a board consisting of all the partners and a general manager

- partners and managers on the board who represent a function as defined above.

There is no single correct organizational structure for general practice; the best one is that which is appropriate to need.


## The doctors, nurses and staff

The implementation of fundholding needs to be clearly identified as the management of change and hence treated as such. Everyone who works in the practice therefore needs to understand what the features of fundholding are and what the practice is trying to achieve.

The collaborative approach is by far the most successful as it allows people to come on board at their own pace and is not considered threatening. People need time to explore their own fears and feelings and to learn about new systems.

### The project or implementation group

Managing the implementation of a change as complex as fundholding requires a specific focus, and this is best done by a small group or working party. This group should ideally consist of:

- one or two GPs
- a manager
- a secretary or data entry clerk.

The group will, in the first instance, have to learn about fundholding, attend various meetings, search out information about computer software, put together a work plan, followed by a business plan. In addition, they will be required to keep the practice personnel informed, provide training and keep a tight rein on practice progress.

## Review of in-house skills (Box 3.3)

This may prove to be one of the most difficult tasks for the project team, but it is a vital requirement. Fundholding requires a variety of management skills:

- communications
- needs assessment
- information systems (IS) and information technology (IT)
- budgeting
- basic accounting
- monitoring
- negotiating
- decision making.

If the practice does not have these skills it will need to recruit a manager who does. As the volume of work increases, a data entry clerk will almost certainly be required. The FHSA fundholding manager is often a rich source of information and advice about recruiting extra staff, who may also suggest using a consultant to supplement the skills deficit. They will also give guidance on how to claim the management allowance which is provided for the purpose of managing the fundholding function.

---

**Box 3.3**

Stage action plan – prepare practice

1 Review present organizational structure and alter as appropriate to need.
2 Appoint a project group to implement the change.
3 Prepare present practice personnel.
4 Recruit additional staff with necessary skills.
5 Set benchmarks and monitor progress.

---

## Computer systems

Part of the entry criteria for the fundholding scheme is that the practice should be computerized. In addition to the clinical system the practice will require a fundholding software program.

Before setting out on a shopping trip it is best to take an in-depth look at the practice's present information technology (IT) and information system (IS). This is time well spent and could save time, effort and money later on. The two key points that should be considered at this stage are:

- What is the present flow of information (both computer and paper) around the practice? A flow chart should be drawn of how many links there are in the chain – for example a doctor dictating a referral letter.
- What IT currently supports this flow of information?

It is obligatory that the practice has a fundholding software program, so modelling how this will best fit in with the above points is a smart way to start. The practice should at this point be considering how the new IT and IS will add value to the administration and operation of patient care and how it will improve the efficiency of the entire practice.

The next stage is to get expert help and advice. Each FHSA or Health Commission has a computer facilitator who can provide the following useful advice.

- Level of reimbursement for all hardware, software and training within that FHSA.

- The advantages/disadvantages of stand-alone systems versus integrated systems.

- Advice on software, hardware, upgrades, maintenance and training.

- Where is the cheapest place to purchase locally, especially if the FHSA has negotiated special deals with suppliers.

- A whole host of matters dependent upon the individual circumstances. For example, multi-users or small practices joining together.

It is strongly recommended that the practice goes through this discipline of review and obtains independent advice before contacting any of the software houses.

Stage three is to draw up a list of hardware requirements:

- hard disk capacity
- number of PCs or terminals
- printers (laser? colour?)
- processor speed
- memory
- silent boxes
- stand-alone or multi-user
- colour user interface
- scanner
- wiring needed
- land line/modems.

Also the software requirements:

- fundholding package
- spreadsheet

- word processing
- database
- links
- accounts
- payroll.

Additional information requirements are:

- What training is needed?
- What level of engineering support is needed?
- Availability of help-line.
- Notifying the Data Protection Department.

Stage four is when the practice has its list of requirements prepared and is now ready to go to the software houses.

Many practices will wish to stay with their present software supplier, but others may want to change. There are at least 11 suppliers of fundholding software; a list is usually published on the directory page of *Fundholding* magazine. There is no right or wrong system; all will have had to obtain accreditation before being approved as suppliers of fundholding software. The guiding principles are to talk to others who use that system, purchase the one that best meets individual needs and remember that computer systems should be an asset and add value to the practice – not be a millstone around the neck (Box 3.4).

---

**Box 3.4**

Action plan

1 Review flow of information around the practice and the IT that supports it.
2 Get expert help and advice.
3 Draw up a list of all your hardware, software and support requirements.
4 Negotiate with computer companies for the practice's requirements.

---

# Information requirements

Information is the lifeblood of the Health Service but far too often it has been stale. Owing to lack of movement it has been allowed to clot and block. Even in the preparatory year the fundholding practice must start managing the quality and movement of information if it is to achieve the full benefits of purchasing for its patients. Like so many other things in this year it is better to start simply and grow with the subject. There are three guiding principles.

- There is no such thing as free information: its collection and collation has a cost – its correct application however, can add value and save money.

- Someone must own the information and its presentation should be according to their specifications.

- The business or practice objectives should drive the information requirements and only that which is necessary should be produced.

## Needs assessment

Needs assessment is the foundation information that every practice requires and its importance cannot be overstated.

Once collated it should form the basis of the business plan, inform the setting of contracts and act as the benchmark for targeting and evaluating effectiveness. Most of the clinical computer systems will produce the information needed in a matter of hours. Consistency and clarity of presentation should be identified at the start. For example:

- total numbers in search
- percentage of practice population
- rate per 1000
- standardized mortality rate (SMR).

*Needs assessment grid*

- health-related behaviours
- excess alcohol consumption

- smokers

- excess weight/body mass

- illicit drug users

- mortality:
  – chronic diseases (asthma, diabetes, bronchitis, hypertension, cerebro-vascular attacks or strokes, hyperlipidaemia, myocardial infarction or angina)
  – cancers (leukaemia, breast, skin, prostate, lung, gastrointestinal)
  – mental illness (neurosis/psychosis, long-term care community maintained)
  – disabilities (learning disabilities, living at home, shared care; and physical disabilities such as multiple sclerosis, post-trauma, hemi-plegia and quadriplegia)

- morbidity:
  – deaths in past 12 months, identified by age
  – ten most common causes of death
  – place of death

- environmental factors:
  – receiving deprivation payments (high, medium, low)
  – living in bed and breakfast accommodation
  – living in residential/nursing homes
  – housebound and unable to attend surgery

- mobility of the population:
  – numbers leaving and joining practice in past 12 months

- age/sex register and ethnic origin.

## Validation of information on needs assessment

Having carried out this extensive needs assessment exercise it is necessary to validate it. Practices exist within a District and it is not likely that the practice population will vary considerably from the district profile, although pockets of deprivation and affluence do exist within a short distance of each other. The best means of validating this information is to compare it against the County Public Health Report. Each District or County Health Commission has a statutory obligation to produce an annual public health report which contains detailed information on the health status of the population. The presentation and content may vary, but generally it is consistent with this needs assessment grid.

It is also useful to compare the practice needs assessment with the national figures which are usually published in the Public Health Report. Marked variations from the district or national norms should be highlighted and may form the benchmark or focus for special attention or additional resource allocation in the next contracting period.

Furthermore, if a practice has gone through this discipline and identified areas of unusual or unmet need it is worthwhile noting it and bringing the facts to the attention of the FHSA fundholding manager and Director of Public Health. It must not be forgotten that the health information held in general practice is probably the most accurate and up to date of all the information databases in the Health Service.

## Complementary information on needs

The practice doctors and nurses who are daily meeting with a large proportion of patients are in an ideal position to contribute to the needs assessment exercise. The computer will only reproduce what has been fed into it and often the infrequent or rare is not systematically recorded. It is always worth asking each clinician what they consider the general and specific health needs of their patients to be.

This is undoubtedly the most important needs assessment the practice will carry out, as it establishes a baseline at the start of fundholding which hopefully information can be measured against in future years. The real value of needs assessment is not its identification but its interpretation and application.

# Epidemiology

Though not all practices may be ready for this level of information in the preparatory year some will be. If the practice had no previous knowledge of usage, etc., it could theoretically build up a picture of likely need based on the study of patterns of disease.

Very briefly, what a practice may wish to know is what is the prevalence of illness (e.g. mental illness) in a population of 10 000 patients in a rural or urban industrial environment. It is also possible to perform disease modelling. Knowing the number of heavy smokers registered with the practice, their state of ill health in say 10 years could be predicted. It is difficult to interpret and transfer these findings to a small population. However, the practice should be aware that such information does exist in Public Health Departments.

### Research findings

Pressure on doctors to make optimum use of scarce resources and from consumer groups to be given a voice in decision making has forced the pace of information on clinical effectiveness. Although the literature on this subject is still varied considerable work is in progress to produce clear, easy-to-use facts about the clinical effectiveness of procedures. In the coming years fundholding practices will be checking out the clinical effectiveness of health care and intervention before signing contracts. In the pursuit of risk reduction it will be in their interest to know about research findings and to have state-of-the-art information on clinical effectiveness.

## Activity levels (see Box 3.5)

By the time the practice has completed the 26-week data collection exercise and carried out its own needs assessment it will have made considerable progress in clarifying what its activity levels are. 'Start simply' is still the best policy and this can always be built upon. The grid shown in Figure 3.2 presented on a flip-chart or spreadsheet can reduce complexity and show a lot of information in a concise format.

Using this format for identifying activity levels, it is possible to maintain consistency and simplicity. If a computer spreadsheet is used it is easy to continue the columns across, inserting variations into each of them and adding the total cost of each service.

In principle there is no difference in measuring activity levels between say ENT out-patients and health visiting. Each service should be encouraged to provide the practice with new referrals/births, visits, etc., the number still on the list or case-load and the number of discharges.

Monitoring the contracts and budget throughout the year is an essential part of fundholding. This continuous activity can be reduced by half if the practice takes care at the start and establishes an activity framework which has the capacity to be updated and fine-tuned. This activity framework has only to be designed once. After that it will facilitate monitoring, guide the business plan and assist with budget setting in future years.

### Capitation

Practices currently entering the fundholding scheme will have their budgets set on the basis of their historical usage of secondary and

| Description of service | New referrals | On waiting list at start of DCP | Treatment completed since start of DCP | Currently on waiting list | Expected activity for 52 wks | Provider prices |
|---|---|---|---|---|---|---|
| Provider A: | | | | | | |
| In-patients/Day -cases: | | | | | | |
| General surgery | | | | | | |
| ENT | | | | | | |
| Urology | | | | | | |
| Gynaecology | | | | | | |
| Trauma and Orth. | | | | | | |
| Ophthalmology | | | | | | |
| Cardiology | | | | | | |
| Others | | | | | | |
| Total in-patients | | | | | | |
| Total day-cases | | | | | | |
| | | | | | | |
| Out-patients: | | | | | | |
| Provider A | | | | | | |
| B | | | | | | |
| C | | | | | | |
| | | | | | | |
| *Diagnosis pathology* | | | | | | |
| Chemical | | | | | | |
| Haematology | | | | | | |
| X-ray | | | | | | |
| Imaging | | | | | | |
| Domiciliary | | | | | | |
| | | | | | | |
| *Direct access* | | | | | | |
| Physiotherapy | | | | | | |
| Speech therapy | | | | | | |
| Dietetics | | | | | | |
| | | | | | | |
| *Community* | | | | | | |
| Health visiting | | | | | | |
| District nursing | | | | | | |
| CPN | | | | | | |
| Chiropody | | | | | | |
| Child & family psychiatry | | | | | | |

**Figure 3.2** An activity spreadsheet grid. DCP = During the 26-week data collection period

community care. For example if the ENT activity level during the preparatory year is:

- out-patients, 100 patients treated

- in-patients, 10 patients treated

- day-cases, 15 patients treated

then the published prices of that provider will be applied to the activity level and this will follow for all other specialties. The activity level multiplied by the provider prices will equal the budget offer.

In 1995–96 regional management executive outposts will move towards establishing a capitation methodology for setting fundholders' budgets. Capitation is based on the principle that it should be possible to build up a budget by identifying the number of patients in the practice, classified by age and gender, and then applying a weighting factor. For example:

> One 85-year-old male   = 2.75 budgetary units
> One 15-year-old female = 0.75 budgetary units

The capitation methodology might be further weighted to reflect local environmental factors such as high deprivation factors. Hence:

> One 85-year-old male   = 3.00 budgetary units
> Living in deprivation zone 20
> One 15-year-old female = 1.00 budgetary units

Likewise, if the practice is in an area which has a high supply of and demand for private health care the methodology may be further adjusted as follows:

> One 85-year-old male   = 1.35 budgetary units
> One 15-year-old female = 0.40 budgetary units

(These figures are for demonstration purposes only and are not intended to be indicative units.)

This principle implies that once the methodology is sufficiently fine-tuned it will be possible to calculate the budgetary requirements of any given fundholding practice, health authority or Region. Its strength will be in its ability to demonstrate without question that all purchasers have been treated equally. The advantage to the fundholding practice lies in the predictability of this methodology. From the time a new patient registers with a practice or someone leaves it, the practice should in theory be able to re-calculate its likely budget for the coming year (subject to inflation adjustments). It should facilitate and permit long-term planning and allow practices to demonstrate the effects of their contracting decisions.

In the interests of equity, access and maximum health gain for the greatest number, it is the wish of every fundholding practice that capitation as a means of constructing a budget will succeed. However, history has shown that despite the best efforts of Regions and Districts, finding the methodology to predict every variable and eventuality in budget setting has repeatedly eluded health-care planners.

---

**Box 3.5**

Action plan

1 Carry out practice needs assessment.

2 Validate the information.

3 Collect other information from clinicians, epidemiology and research findings.

4 Design a practice activity framework.

5 Start enquiring about capitation methodology in your region, including introduction date.

---

4　The Management Allowance

*David and Pat Archer*

## Introduction

The management allowance is a payment that may be made in re-imbursement of extra expenditure incurred by a practice undertaking fundholding work. This may be preparatory work in the year leading up to fundholding or work in managing a fund. Two or more practices may join together for the purpose of fundholding and are then treated as one practice and are eligible for only one allowance. The allowance is not a flat-rate fee and is paid as reimbursement of actual additional costs incurred. The maximum levels of management allowance from 1 April 1993 are as follows:

- Preparatory year £17,500
- Preparatory year (grouped fundholder) £20,000
- Fundholding year £35,000
- Locum element £3,718.

Maximum limits on capital expenditure:

– Capital expenditure (preparatory year), 50% of the maximum allowance

– Capital expenditure (full year), 25% of the maximum allowance.

There is no increase from 1 April 1994. At the time of writing the latest regulations are set out in HSG(93)43 published 23 August 1993. A management allowance is payable to:

- a single practice with a list size of more than 7000 patients

- two or more practices with list sizes less than 7000 each but with a joint list size of more than 7000

- two or more practices where one practice has a list size of more than 7000 patients and the other practices in the group have individual list sizes of less than 7000 patients.

A management allowance is not payable to a group of two or more practices, each of which have list sizes of more than 7000 patients, except where such practices manage their own separate funds as part of a 'consortium' of fundholding practices.


# Who is eligible and the business plan

The criteria for acceptance for the scheme are laid down in Schedule 1 of the NHS (Fundholding Practices) Regulations 1993; more information is given elsewhere in this book. A practice or group of practices authorized by the responsible RHA to take on preparatory work will prepare a business plan for the best way to prepare for managing a fund from the following April. The plan will include details of how it is intended to use the management allowance and must be agreed with the RHA or Family Health Services Authority (FHSA) depending on local arrangements, although increasingly in practice this means the FHSA. The practice or fundholding group may then claim full reimbursement of expenses set out in the business plan as they occur. The plan should not be inflexible and details may be revised by agreement. During the preparatory year the preparation may be more expensive for a group of practices, hence a group may claim to a higher maximum than a single practice.

When a practice or group of practices has been recognized as a fundholding practice it should present an outline plan of the additional expenses that will come from managing a fund. The plan should be submitted to the FHSA for approval by the end of the financial year before the year covered by the plan.

The preparation of a business plan is dealt with elsewhere. However, it would be prudent when considering how the management allowance will be used to build in an element for the unexpected by including a reserve. In other words do not plan to spend it all. If there are any doubts as to what to include it can only be helpful to discuss the matter with the FHSA. Allowance that is not spent in one year cannot be carried forward into the next year.

# Withdrawal from the scheme

In the event that a practice withdraws from the preparatory phase or from the scheme there is no requirement to repay any of the reimbursements already made. Any expenditure made up to the date of withdrawal will be paid.

# Uses and abuses

The intention is that the management allowance should cover additional expenditure that has to be made to make fundholding work. The main headings for examples of expenses that may be reimbursed are:

- employment of staff to manage the fund
- employment of staff to retrieve data for fundholding
- use of locum services to cover partners' absences when engaged in fundholding business
- undertaking any other work necessary in the preparatory year
- training relevant to fundholding for practice staff or GPs
- buying in specialist advice
- purchase of equipment to help in the management of the fund.

Each practice or group will decide on the structure of management that will best suit their own circumstances. Staff are needed to manage fundholding, to capture data to determine treatment and referral patterns, to enter data on the computer system, to prepare reports and to monitor fundholding. The fund manager will probably be included in the process of contracting and the monitoring of contracts with providers. A member of staff will probably spend time checking that claims from providers for payment represent work actually performed and if necessary investigating discrepancies with the provider. The expenses of employing staff to undertake this work are all reimbursable at 100% of the cost of pay and employer's National Insurance contributions. Staff costs will be the major claim on the management allowance.

A member of staff employed to assist with the delivery of general medical services may in addition be employed for fundholding purposes but of course only that part of the costs that results from fundholding can be borne by the management allowance. If the practice manager works extra time to prepare for or to manage fundholding then payment for that time can be a charge on the management allowance. Another example would be if a practice data clerk spends some hours recording fundholding data or secretarial staff spend time on fundholding. The costs of their pay for fundholding duties can then be claimed against the allowance. It is most important to identify clearly which costs are attributable to fundholding activities, as there is the potential for abuse and consequently the claim is subject to audit.

Reimbursement is allowed for employing locum services to allow a GP to spend time on work necessary to manage a fund. During the preparatory year if the partners cover for the partner who is undertaking the additional work instead of employing a locum the practice may claim the locum allowance as a payment to the practice in recognition of the additional hours worked. However in subsequent years managing a fund the locum allowance cannot be claimed unless a locum is actually employed.

Anything that improves the collection of data in the preparatory year is worth while and provided it meets the criteria outlined in this chapter will be allowable.

Properly instructed staff will be much more effective and a good business plan will incorporate an allowance for training staff. Claims may consist of fees for any member of the fundholding staff to attend a course directly concerned with fundholding. As a minimum it would be wise for fundholding staff to attend a course on operating the software. This comprises not only basic data entry but the ability to produce regular reports detailing fundholding activity and to do all that is necessary for year-end closure. A practice or fund manager might claim the cost of a course in understanding the principles of accountancy, or a GP could claim for a course in negotiating skills.

The fees for buying in specialist advice and business consultancy are allowable against the management allowance. Such advice is often expensive. Practices may wish to bear in mind that much can be done in-house and that advice is available from other fundholders and local groups of fundholders. Many FHSAs offer advice and courses.

The management allowance may be used to purchase equipment necessary for the management of the fund. Equipment that may be required ranges from computers, fax machine, photocopier and other office equipment to telephone lines or office furniture for use by fundholding staff. There are limits to how much can be spent on capital items: 50% of the maximum allowance in the preparatory year and 25% in a full year.

It should not be forgotten that the costs of installing, running and maintaining the equipment are a legitimate claim on the allowance. These costs may extend from wiring for the fundholding computer, consumable items such as paper, to rental for the telephone or fax line. Where a facility is shared only that part of the expense that is attributable to fundholding can be claimed against the allowance. An example would be where a telephone line is not used exclusively for the administration of fundholding.

The allowance cannot be used to reimburse costs incurred in building extensions or making modifications to surgery premises to accommodate additional staff employed for fundholding. In addition claims cannot be made for the same expenses against the management allowance and under any arrangements in the Statement of Fees and Allowances.

## Claiming

The FHSA is responsible for receiving claims and making payment once the RHA or FHSA and the practice have agreed a budget plan for use of the management allowance. In cases where the FHSA is initially responsible for agreeing the plan it should also be approved by the RHA. The responsible FHSA will provide forms on which claims on the preparatory or management allowances may be made. An example of a form is shown in Figure 4.1. The claim is submitted to the FHSA with proof of expenditure being incurred or confirmation of payment.

The FHSA has the task of monitoring and accounting for the allowances and so will check that the claim is for an agreed expense before making the reimbursement. If the practice is in any doubt as to whether an item of expenditure will be allowed it makes sense to discuss the proposed purchase before the practice enters into any financial commitment. The outlay may be allowed under the regulations but not under the approved plan; it may then be necessary to submit a new (modified) plan for approval. The FHSA will probably provide a monthly statement of claims made against the allowance showing accumulated expenditure. A monthly statement might appear as in Table 4.1.

Because the allowances are reimbursement of costs that have been actually incurred and paid, the regulations do not allow payment on account by equal monthly instalments of the maximum expected amount as shown in the plan. However, in the case of regular recurrent expenditure such as salaries the FHSA may make payment on account and will expect that the practice will later provide proof that the claim is valid.

GP FUNDHOLDING: MANAGEMENT ALLOWANCE
APPLICATION FOR PAYMENT

**Details of Practice**

Name of Doctor, partnership or group ......................................
(practice stamp)

**Details of Costs for the month of**           ....................

a) Employment of Staff           £ ....................
b) Staff Training Costs          £ ....................
c) Locum Cover                   £ ....................
d) Equipment                     £ ....................
e) Consumables                   £ ....................
f) Bought in Management          £ ....................
g) Others                        £ ....................

Total                            £ ....................

Please attach proof of payment

**Declaration**

I/We apply for direct imbursement of the above items of management
expenditure which have been incurred in preparation for fundholding
by this practice

Doctor's signature ......................................... Date ...............

**Official Use Only**      Management Allowance   £
                           Spend to Date          £
                           This claim             £
                           Spend C/F

Authorised for payment  .................................... Date ...............

**Figure 4.1** GP fundholding management allowance application form

**Table 4.1** Monthly balance sheet

GP FUNDHOLDING: MANAGEMENT ALLOWANCE 1994/95

Dr Smith & Partners
The Surgery
18 Main Road
Any Town

| DETAILS | APR | MAY | JUN | JUL | AUG | SEPT | OCT | NOV | DEC | JAN | FEB | MAR | TOTAL | PLAN TOTAL |
|---|---|---|---|---|---|---|---|---|---|---|---|---|---|---|
| EMPLOYMENT OF STAFF | 2 033 | 2 033 | 2 033 | 2 124 | 2 136 | 2 230 | 2 235 | 2 235 | 2 036 | 2 035 | | | 18 141 | 25 800 |
| STAFF TRAINING | 185 | 60 | 0 | 150 | 0 | 0 | 85 | 0 | 135 | 295 | | | 1 010 | 1 500 |
| LOCUM COVER | 305 | 305 | 280 | 250 | 320 | 320 | 320 | 320 | 320 | 320 | | | 3 020 | 3 700 |
| BOUGHT IN SERVICES | 0 | 0 | 500 | 0 | 0 | 0 | 100 | 0 | 0 | 0 | | | 600 | 1 500 |
| OTHER | 0 | 80 | 356 | 342 | 48 | 0 | 326 | 581 | 125 | 50 | | | 1 908 | 2 500 |
| MONTHLY TOTAL | 2 523 | 2 578 | 3 169 | 2 896 | 2 434 | 2 550 | 3 066 | 3 136 | 2 816 | 2 900 | | | 28 068 | 35 000 |

Payment of expenses allowed and the reimbursement for these expenses should be made through a separate bank account opened for the sole purpose of operating the management allowance.

## Management allowance and practice accounts

The management allowance is income of the practice and so must be shown in the practice accounts. It is important to determine which is capital expenditure and which is revenue expenditure. Then income which reflects reimbursement from the management allowance to cover non-capital expenditure will be matched by revenue expenditure in the profit and loss account and so there will be no liability to payment of income tax. Capital expenditure can be brought in as additions to fixed assets with a deduction for that part of the purchase that was financed from the management allowance and thus again there will be no liability to payment of income tax.

The partnership may wish to consider how it wishes these assets to be treated for the purposes of partnership capital. One possibility on the retirement of a partner or the entry of a new partner would be to have the assets valued. An alternative might be to use written-down values. The partnership agreement may need to be brought up to date to reflect how the partnership wishes to treat assets acquired under fundholding.

## Problems with the allowance

The management allowance was set in the early days of fundholding, when criteria for acceptance as a fundholding practice included a higher list size, so that practices were of a similar size and an allowance of the same amount for each practice had some merit. However, fundholding practices can now have a list size from just over 7000 to more than 20 000 and there are now consortia of fundholding practices. Larger practices have to handle more data. It is uncertain to what extent these extra costs might be offset by economies of scale in other areas of management but it is certain that the management costs of such diverse practices and groups of practices are different. Fortunately, the Management Executive is reviewing the problem in response to pressure from fundholders for a variable allowance related to practice size.

The second major problem perceived by fundholders is that there is no recognition of the time that has to be given to fundholding by the lead partner. If the most is to be made of the opportunities presented by fundholding much effort and time has to be expended on fundholding. A claim against the management allowance, other than for a locum, is allowed only in the preparatory year. This is a source of concern to many fundholders, and it is to be hoped that this problem will be addressed by the Management Executive.

# 5 The Role of the Fund Manager

## Stephen Jones

Inevitably, fundholding will bring new tasks and additional work to the practice. When a practice becomes a fundholder it takes on specific responsibilities. These include:

- a commissioning role

- a health-planning function

- custodianship of public funds and the preparation of certified annual accounts

- negotiation of service level agreements for patient services

- ensuring the accuracy of data entered onto the GPFH computer system

- regularly reporting on finance and activity to the FHSA

- monitoring the performance of hospital providers and its own fund

- being publicly accountable for its actions.

Any partnership will probably not wish to absorb this extra workload unaided, and this chapter examines the role of the fund manager in the context of these new responsibilities, as suitable management resources are critical to success in fundholding.

The practice may already have the necessary skills within the team or they may be provided by arrangement with the Family Health Services Authority (FHSA). If not, then it will be necessary to recruit a suitably qualified person. This is a critical appointment, and it could be costly to the practice in both financial and human terms if it were to make an inappropriate selection.

The role of the fund manager should be to predict, calculate, interpret and explain the financial implications of changes brought about by clinical decision making and to facilitate the discharge of the above responsibilities. The effect of this will be to integrate business/health planning into the delivery of care such that the partners have access to all necessary information on financial outcomes prior to making decisions in their clinical role.

## The qualifications and qualities of a fund manager

Fundholding is a development still in its infancy, one which requires a structured yet open-minded approach to its operation. To function effectively in the role, a fund manager should be prepared to work under a range of pressures. The possession of a high standard of general intelligence, an ability to communicate orally and in writing and good numerical ability are requisite personal attributes. As a representative for both the practice and its patients, the manager should create a strong impression. About 5 years' health-service experience, preferably in primary health care, would seem to offer a sound understanding of the current environment in the NHS.

In terms of education, the fund manager may well possess a relevant degree in management, accounting, or similar professional qualification and may have attained this on a part-time basis while in employment. Arguably more important than formal qualifications is proven managerial experience in a multi-professional organization. The ability to plan, organize, co-ordinate and control and work under pressure are key skills. It would be desirable for the incumbent to be familiar with financial management in the public sector, while a working knowledge of computerized systems in general practice would be clearly advantageous.

The fund manager should be motivated to achieve and to influence others effectively. Clearly, the ability to adjust, to innovate and to manage change is important, as is a sense of vision towards the practice's strategic goals. These attributes are normally associated with a mature and stable personality, demonstrating strong leadership and management skills. An ability to communicate at all levels and to be persuasive in argument, through excellent influencing skills, is crucial.

The availability of a fund manager in the practice can add to the analytical, change management and 'political' skills of the team. By freeing the GP to contemplate implementation and development issues, the fund manager enhances the practice's status/credibility as a commissioner of health care and reinforces control, centralized co-ordination and communication within the practice. Once in post, the fund manager will need to guide and support the partnership to meet the responsibilities listed above. It is unlikely that anyone will initially possess all the necessary skills and some thought therefore needs to be given to the fund manager's training needs.

The daily running of the fund, practice/provider relationships and the preparation of a health (business) plan are discussed later in this chapter. Other areas where skills will be required include the writing of service agreements, monitoring provider quality and the management of waiting lists. Aspects of financial management, such as the monitoring of performance against budget or making virement decisions, may require training in the use of spreadsheet models to supplement the information provided by the fundholding computer system. A comprehensive understanding of the fundholding software is vital and the need for the system supplier to provide training and support in this area cannot be overstressed. This becomes particularly important when the 'end of year' procedures have to be implemented to produce the annual accounts.

## The partner/fund manager relationship

An effective fund manager should allow the GPs, as the 'owners' of the fund, to take a more strategic view of their purchaser role. In this context, strategic vision is about the GP making a cultural leap from the clinical management of individuals to the commissioning of specific services for the whole practice population. In doing so, the nature of the GPs' role will change. The nature of issues will become more abstract and judgemental as the GPs' place on the decision making continuum shifts from individual to population care planning and it is in this aspect that an effective manager can best support GPs.

In this new strategic role, the GP finds himself faced with difficult and complex managerial and organizational issues which are often an uncomfortable 'fit' with clinical practice. There is often a problem of coping with the complexity of the commissioning process and deciding on what basis to make choices. This is not to imply that GPs are incapable of understanding the process, merely recognizing that there is an enormous amount to grasp. Involvement in the fine detail of commissioning would not necessarily be a good use of a GP's time.

| Managerial decisions | |
|---|---|
| Operational issues (individual patient care) | Strategic issues (practice level commissioning) |
| • routine<br>• closed decisions<br>• good data/information available<br>• short-term/urgent matters | • non-routine<br>• open systems<br>• require 'conceptualization'<br>• increased 'bureaucracy'<br>• long-term view |

The partnership should delegate when there is more work than can be effectively carried out by partners alone, when it is not possible to allow sufficient time for identified priority tasks, or when the job can be done adequately by the fund manager. When considering the range of fund staff the practice needs, it will be necessary to prepare job descriptions and person specifications, which can only be constructed once the partners/lead GP have determined the relationship they require with the fund manager/staff together with the level of *delegation* that is appropriate. Delegation may be defined as 'giving others the authority to act on your behalf, accompanying it with responsibility and accountability for results', where authority is the right to make decisions, take actions and give orders. Responsibility relates to the job and/or tasks the incumbent is given to do, and accountability is the fund manager's liability to the partnership and his obligation to accept responsibility and use authority.

Delegation is important as it:

- relieves GPs of routine and less critical fundholding tasks and frees them for more important work such as clinical practice or the planning, organizing, and control of commissioning activity

- extends the capacity to manage the practice fund

- reduces delay in decision making, as long as authority is delegated close to the point of action

- allows decisions to be taken at the level where the details are known.

Once the partnership has decided to delegate specific fund management matters, both parties need to understand:

- what the fund manager/staff are expected to do

- the authority devolved to make decisions
- the problems/issues that must be referred back to the partnership
- the financial and activity reports that must be submitted to various interested parties and the timescale
- the basis for monitoring performance, i.e. what constitutes success or failure?
- the resources and help that will be required or available to get the work done.

When examining the potential for successful delegation of management of the practice fund, it is worth considering how the process will work. Thought should be given to the allocation of responsibility for specific aspects of fundholding amongst the partners, such as a partner responsible for negotiations with a particular provider, or for producing a formulary/clinical guidelines in a particular therapeutic group. Therefore, an analysis of individual partner skills and interest should be undertaken to derive:

- an agreed statement of expertise, abilities and role preferences of individual partners
- an estimate of activity time, analysed between different fund management activities and including expected growth in the demands of fundholding
- development goal statements by individual partners.

The end result of this process should ensure that the respective roles of partner and fund manager are clear and complementary. This allows the manager to concentrate on the successful and efficient implementation of fund management within the practice organization by establishing appropriate and necessary monitoring arrangements and reviewing the management controls.

# The fund manager's contribution to the commissioning role

As a commissioner of health care, the fundholding practice will negotiate with provider hospitals. The way in which the practice negotiating team is constructed plays an important part in the success of all such negotiations. It will help considerably if one partner takes on the executive responsibility for fundholding. Not only is some clinical input invaluable for effective negotiations, but it encourages the development of a sound and productive relationship between the partnership and management. The lead GP and fund manager often negotiate as a team, where they act as the practice representatives. The process of negotiation may be quite complex and it is suggested that the practice has such a negotiating team, which might be as small as two people, or possibly as large as four. Once it gets beyond this number it is difficult to manage and some team members will appear to take no part in the negotiation. The practice may wish to have a different team for each provider, by alternating the GP representative, where existing GP/consultant relationships may enhance the process.

When preparing for negotiations it is useful for one team member to act as a devil's advocate. This will indicate potential weaknesses in your own arguments and develop a strong commitment to the practice's negotiating position. Sometimes negotiating teams develop a cosy atmosphere and become unwilling to discuss the potential weaknesses of their arguments, fearing that this may upset other team colleagues. This has been called 'group think' and, by legitimizing the role of devil's advocate, group think is avoided. Another valuable feature of having more than one person involved in negotiations is that different styles can be used. At a simple level this could be the fund manager taking a hard line, while the GP takes a much softer line, or vice versa.

It should be remembered that the responsibility to plan, individually and collectively, the commissioning of secondary clinical activity (to provide for the identified level of health care necessary for the practice's patients) remains that of the partnership.

## Building relationships outside the practice

It is worthwhile considering the roles of the practice's partners in fundholding. These include the RHA, the FHSA, the DHA, NHS Trusts and directly managed units.

The RHA has overall responsibility for the effective operation of the fundholding scheme, and in this role it:

• assesses practices' suitability for fundholding status

• conciliates in contractual disputes between practices and providers

- determines the value of the fund allocated to the practice

- approves expenditure for the preparatory year fee and management allowance

- is a source of advice and guidance to fundholders in their purchasing role.

In some Regions, and in Wales where there is no RHA, much of this role has been delegated to the FHSAs. The FHSAs (and their equivalents in Scotland and Northern Ireland) continue to exercise their current responsibilities in relation to all GPs for delivery of health care with respect to general medical services. In addition, they have new responsibilities in relation to fundholding, including the following:

- holding fundholders' budgets and paying invoices on their behalf

- routine monitoring of fundholder expenditure, as each practice is required to submit every month a number of reports covering expenditure and activity to the FHSA. The FHSA submits a summary of these reports to the RHA

- advising the RHA on practices' initial and continuing suitability for fundholding status

- calculating the staff and prescribing elements of the fund

- validation of both preparatory year fee and management allowance expenditure and reimbursing fundholders for relevant computer costs.

The fund manager should hold regular meetings with the FHSA to discuss fundholding performance and will also instigate much of the source documentation by which the FHSA monitor the practice.

The DHA and fundholding practices have no direct relationship with one another, but both are searching for high-quality and cost-effective health care for their respective populations. This detachment is becoming less clear as DHAs and FHSAs increase their level of joint working. Fundholding covers only a limited range of services, and the DHA remains responsible for purchasing health-care services that are provided to the practice's patients outside the scope of the fund.

As joint purchasers or commissioners of health care, it is worth practices and the DHA/FHSA examining common interests in relation to particular providers, such as quality and innovative methods of service delivery. The fund manager must advise the DHA when patients approach or exceed the financial threshold for hospital services in the fund, as the DHA is liable to pay for treatment costs in excess of this.

The relationship between practices and NHS Trusts or directly managed units is the cornerstone of the NHS reforms. If any improvements are to be made to service delivery, they must be brought about by influencing this relationship. The fund manager, in daily contact with providers, can make a key contribution to the development of the relationship. To realize the benefits to patient services that follow from becoming a fundholder, it is necessary to work closely with providers. In this way it will be possible to explore jointly possibilities for purchase/delivery of new services and a re-examination of the methods of providing existing services. This may involve an extensive process of option appraisal, to which the fund manager is able to devote more time than the GP, especially if the practice believes service improvements may only be possible if the nature and/or location of their delivery is changed. The fund manager is uniquely placed to encourage a collaborative yet flexible approach in the planning and contracting processes.

## What the fund manager's job involves

For all types of fundholders the manager will be involved in the following:

- Integrating the elements of the fund with practice clinical policy (which must be based on a sound understanding of the mechanisms by which the fund has been derived and the reasons and logic which underpin clinical decision making) and arranging virement between elements, as required.

- Undertaking such detailed negotiations with the FHSA (in respect of the staff and drugs elements of the fund) and with the DHA/RHA (in respect of the diagnostic, hospital and community nursing elements of the fund) as the partners may delegate.

- Preparation and reconciliation of fund accounts for partnership approval, prior to payment.

- Establishing, with the partners, the terms of the service agreements with provider hospitals and devising mechanisms for effective monitoring and review. This will also mean examination of alternative sources of supply.

- Examining invoices for accuracy and initial investigation of discrepancies.

- Preparing such regular and *ad hoc* reports as may be necessary for the effective management and audit of fund activity.

Irrespective of whether individuals or combined funds are involved, the fund manager will have to introduce systems and procedures:

- To create, amend and maintain the fundholding system database in respect of all hospital referral activities, including:

  - setting up of providers' details on computer system
  - creation of service agreements, recognizing referral protocols and practices
  - access to current pricing data.

- Reconciling activity reported by practice and by provider such that any discrepancies are resolved to the satisfaction of the practice. It will be necessary to validate that all patient activity is recognized by the system.

- To allow for daily operation of both the referral and nominal ledgers (i.e. activity, invoicing and payment systems). This will also involve closing monthly or other period accounts and producing reports, as required.

- To monitor financial performance of the staff element of fundholding, by reference to payroll costs and authorized budget, to prepare reconciliations and investigate discrepancies.

- To monitor financial and prescribing performance of the practice in relation to the authorized budget for the drugs and appliances element of fundholding.

- To ensure that the fundholding computer system operates at optimal performance and that users are aware of amendments/updates/developments as necessary, also maintaining relevant system error, fault and repair logs. In addition, this will involve ensuring the security of the system, including password access to various levels of the system, the taking and storage of tape back-ups of system data and the physical security/integrity of the system.

Individual fundholding practices may wish to co-operate and form management consortia in order to more effectively perform such activities as planning and contracting. While this allows practices to achieve the advantages of greater influence over providers during the contracting process, through economies of scale and the exchange of ideas for service developments, it may complicate the management task. Working with other fundholders in a commissioning consortium allows practices to become a significant force for change in discussions with both hospital clinicians and managers. Alternatively, where practices do not meet the size criteria for fundholding recognition in their own right, they may combine with another practice to become a single fundholder, and this makes the fund manager's role much more challenging. For practices combining to hold one fund, it must be remembered that the fund is a single entity distributed between combining practices.

In a fundholder combined from two or more practices, the typical role of the manager will also probably include:

- formulating the agreement which confirms that any act by a member in relation to the fund binds the other members of the combining practices

- reaching an agreement on the notional apportionment of the fund between practices and encouraging policies for prescribing and contracting which are common to each of the practices

- formulating procedures that will be followed in the event of one member overspending their notional part of (or indeed the overall) fund.

Just as delegation of certain functions from partner to manager is appropriate, it follows that data entry staff are essential to input patient activity information into the fundholding system. One aspect of fundholding that has been generally underestimated is the volume of activity data that must be captured for effective management of the fund. It is clearly not resource- or time-effective for a fund manager to undertake this aspect and well-trained support staff are vital to the practical operation of the system.

## Health planning and the fund manager

Health plans, business plans, fundholding plans and development plans are terms often erroneously used interchangeably. While their individual purpose may differ, the process and contents are often similar. Health planning is one of the new responsibilities devolved to GP fundholders and can be considered to be the decision-making process concerned with managing change to ensure the better provision of future services. The preparation of the annual health plan is a key component of the fund manager's role. Individual sections could be separately written provided a co-ordinator remains in overall editorial control of the text. The health plan is not meant to be a voluminous document and should be as concise as possible, consistent with its purpose. It should be remembered that fine detail needs to be consigned to appendices, leaving the main plan as a comprehensive statement.

The process consists of analysing the current situation, formulating practice objectives and deciding on strategies and tactics to bring them to fruition. Fundholding seems to have initiated a gradual change in the general view of GPs with regard to planning, clinical care and resource availability. They are now able to appreciate the greater need for effective and efficient planning in less affluent circumstances. The fund manager's objectives will therefore include the creation of an appropriate information system. With such information readily accessible, the fund manager is well placed to commence drafting the practice health plan. The health plan is about the management of the fund, so it is important that all the partners contribute to and convey their enthusiasm and commitment to it. It may be appropriate to involve other staff in its creation, such as the practice manager or fundholding support staff, but while others may contribute, the setting of practice goals must ultimately remain the responsibility of the partners.

General practice fundholding covers only part of the overall delivery of health care services to practice patients and currently relates to the following distinct areas:

- referrals to consultant out-patient services
- certain elective procedures in a discrete number of specialties, provided on both in-patient and day-case bases
- defined direct access services, such as physiotherapy
- diagnostic tests and investigations, such as X-rays
- domiciliary consultant visits
- community nursing services.

In planning terms, commissioners are encouraged to shift purchasing towards the delivery of *health gain*. The phraseology used in health planning tends to change on a regular basis and one of the most recent concepts is that of health gain. This concept encourages fundholders to consider how their commissioning role, in combination with the general medical and other services provided by the practice, will ensure that all patient contacts directed by the practice are:

- *health gain focused* – adding years to life through reduction of risk factors contributing to premature death, and life to years by promoting individual awareness and encouraging improvement in well-being

- *patient centred* – valuing patients as individuals and managing services to provide the optimum care that each individual requires to the highest standard achievable; and

- *resource effective* – as far as the practice is able and as is compatible with its commissioning objectives and clinical responsibilities, to deploy resources cost-effectively.

The health plan should relate only to the six discrete areas mentioned above. To avoid adverse change affecting provider units, the practice may wish to continue to contract with its existing providers in the main and any shift in commissioning should be preceded by notice of intention to existing providers. Changes proposed by fundholders are often marginal in cost terms, but offer significant health gains for patients and provide measurable alternative delivery mechanisms, although the benefits may not accrue in the same financial year.

Waiting-list management is a clear success criterion for fundholders and must comprise one of the key health plan objectives. Provider hospitals should be able to provide the practice with detailed data about the practice waiting list. A full analysis of patients on out-patient and in-patient waiting lists should be performed on a regular basis and analysed by the provider. This information can be used to monitor the achievement of the Patient's Charter guarantees and, hopefully, information technology systems at provider units will permit a comprehensive waiting-list validation to take place on at least a quarterly basis.

The practice will have, perhaps limited, information on the number of patients and times of waiting on various waiting lists but this may not be sufficient to construct an overall picture. With regard to in-patients and day-case patients, for example, some providers may be unable to distinguish between chargeable and non-chargeable procedures. Therefore, both practice and health authority (i.e. all commissioners') waiting lists may be subject to an undetermined margin of error due to this. The fund manager will need to accommodate this and similar variables into the planning process.

Each practice should, as part of its planning activity, continue to review the benefits and costs of general practice fundholding status for both the patients and the GPs. The following are typical objectives which may underpin a practice's commissioning strategy.

- Provision of a comprehensive preventive, curative and palliative health care service for its patients.

- Maintaining and improving the quality of its existing secondary health care services, while supporting innovative and appropriate methods for the delivery of health care to its patients.

- Playing an important part in the development of local strategies for health and the measurement of health gain, as a joint commissioner.

- Balancing the competing objectives of providing optimum health care services with that of achieving improved cost control.

- Extending and developing its relationships with secondary care clinicians, other GP fundholders, the RHA, the FHSA, the DHA, provider units and NHS Trusts.

The purpose behind fundholder health plans is the development of a set of common goals and objectives to which the GPs and fellow DHA/ FHSA commissioners are committed. This requires the fullest information on the cost, quality, quantity and availability of the essential components of various clinical procedures and services.

Even though each fundholding practice is unique and plans are written for specific purposes, a standard plan format with essential elements is often expected. This ensures that all the significant matters are addressed in turn, yet still allows the creation of a document which is particular to the practice. If a similar format is adopted it makes it easy for the plan to be followed and the sections normally included, in their order of appearance, would be:

- the *index*, which is the guide to what is to follow

- a *summary or overview* of the plan, to attract the reader to finish the document

- the *purpose* of the plan, which makes clear the reasons for preparing the plan

- the *history* and details of the practice, showing the practice is capable of managing change
- development *proposals*, which quantify the purpose in terms of time and resources
- summarized *commissioning information*, confirming that the fuller implications have been thought through; and
- supporting *appendices*, leaving the above sections free of detailed information.

It is useful to now examine each of these sections in a little more detail.

## The index

This is the guide which takes the reader logically through the plan. It is not so important how the plan is indexed as long as it has one logical structure which allows the reader to see at a glance what the plan contains and where individual items of information are located. This allows for ready cross-referencing and avoids the need to duplicate information unnecessarily.

## The summary/overview

Often called an executive summary, it is meant to be an extract of the document. It should be concise but must be written in a way that is sufficiently attractive to make the reader want to read the whole of the document. These first two sections cannot be actually written until the rest of the document has been virtually completed. It is, however, possible for the fund manager to develop a skeleton framework for these sections to ensure that key points are brought to the fore.

## Statement of purpose

This is where the principal aim of the plan is developed and formulated. Everything else provides supporting information to secure that aim. By giving the reader a concise statement of purpose, further examination of the details will be undertaken with the overall goals clearly in mind. When preparing a purchasing/health plan, the fund manager should remember that this involves the utilization of scarce NHS resources and it is therefore important to:

- quantify these

- state the function to which they will be put
- make an assessment of the benefits that will accrue to all parties from this course of action.

Clearly, financial outcomes will be more easily measured than improvements to health, but the imperfections in the outcome measures need not detract from making sensible predictions. The plan needs to demonstrate that the partners, or perhaps the extended primary health care team, have the abilities to successfully manage the practice(s) as a fundholder.

## Practice details

This section is the opportunity to provide more details on the practice. In particular, the fund manager should outline the current distribution of secondary care services provided to the practice and the financial arrangements underpinning this. The intention is to provide the reader with sufficient information to understand how and why the practice has reached its present position. This should therefore not be expansive, but sufficient to convey the key points. Historical data need to be readily to hand to prepare the details which allow an evaluation of where the practice is now and how it arrived there.

## Development proposals

To this point, the document has detailed the practice history, current position, and the goal(s) aimed for. This section involves projecting present and proposed services into the future. It is therefore that much more difficult for the fund manager to write as the underlying assumptions will be subject to careful, and public, scrutiny. Proposed developments should be shown to be appropriate, realistic and credible. Remember that in producing a plan for the future, the fund manager needs to demonstrate that the practice is capable of achieving the proposed goals. Goals need to be:

- objective
- measurable
- achievable.

Having identified where the practice is and where the partners want it to be, it is necessary to set goals against which achievement/success as a fundholder can be measured and, in doing so, the fund manager will need to estimate the resources and changes needed to achieve the plan. The plan will be more likely to succeed if the fund manager considers some of the questions that may be raised.

- Are the plans achievable/worthwhile?

- What are the long-term effects of failing to implement the plans?

- Do the financial forecasts support the proposals?

- Are the assumptions conservative/optimistic?

- Have alternative options to the proposal been considered?

Considering these in advance may save the fund manager considerable effort later on and helps the production of an effective narrative. The narrative is equally as, if not more important than, the figures or schedules, and these need to be consistent with one another. This allows the practice the opportunity to state its case and justify the use of the underlying assumptions.

The annual health plan often requires specific components, the data from which are then aggregated at the FHSA level. As the health plan is geared to reviewing the practice and the population it serves, the range of services currently provided is often supported by a limited number of key practice development objectives. The text has to include a detailed breakdown of purchasing intentions, proposals for the management of the prescribing element of the fund, and action plans for each of the key initiatives that have been decided on by the partners.

## Summarized financial information

This section may be limited to an analysis of the calculation and disbursement of the fund, but it should only include the information which is relevant to the development proposals. Simply including contract summaries may not be adequate, as it is important that the financial implications are properly interpreted by the reader, in order to convey the correct message. The fund has been derived from historic data and is the basis on which to build the projections into the future.

This may be the area where some support is required from a specialist health planner. If the practice has computer software that allows spreadsheet models to be created, then the fund manager may make a start which can be later refined. The advantage of spreadsheet modelling is that a number of scenarios, based on various input factors, can be developed without laborious workings by hand. Where produced, these should include a commentary on their interpretation. Essentially, this section should summarize the forecasts and key assumptions, so detailed projections should be consigned to an appendix. It should be remembered that it *is* a projection into the future, and need not be calculated to the last pound!

## Supporting appendices

The fund manager should use this section to include all the relevant detail which supports the assumptions, analysis and predictions included in the previous section. It will inevitably be different for each practice and the fund manager must judge what is appropriate to include. This section should not be used to 'pad out' the plan, so only that which is directly relevant to the other sections of the plan should be included.

# Conclusion

At the beginning of this chapter some of the responsibilities that have to be assumed by the new fundholder were listed. The following areas have been identified as key components to being a successful fundholder:

- commissioning
- building relationships
- health planning
- budgetary control
- systems set-up.

It is clear from the breadth and diversity of the management task necessary for the effective discharge of these responsibilities that, in most practices, most functions will be the responsibility of the fund manager. The contribution made by the fund manager is therefore key to success in fundholding. The nature of the role places the fund manager at the forefront of change management in the NHS and the greater challenge of improving services for patients.

# 6    The Fund (Budget)

## John Ellis, Jenny Griffiths, Willie Sime and John Wilkinson

## Introduction

The advent of fundholding has led for the first time in the history of the NHS to the setting of budgets at practice level. Given the size of the undertaking, not suprisingly a few initial difficulties have arisen.

Whilst DHA purchasers are now subject to a formula-based resource allocation process focused on an amount per head of population (capitation) arrived at once several factors have been taken into account (weighted), such as the proportion of elderly people, fundholder budgets remain unique in that:

- they are *negotiated* not allocated (partly because the fundholding scheme remains voluntary)

- the hospital budget is based on a historical count of activity multiplied by price of services purchased as published by providers

- drug budgets are cash limited, not just indicative, and are based principally on historical spending patterns.

A move towards weighted capitation for fundholders seems inevitable, but is far more complex than at first sight because of the huge, and still not fully explained, variation in referral rates to hospital between individual GPs (likely to be a three- or four-fold variation between high and low referrers[1]) and in GPs' prescribing practice. Research suggests that these variations are likely to reflect differences in practitioners' individual referral thresholds, rather than differences in patient populations, facilities and services or in-practice characteristics.

An unresearched interface exists between the various elements of the budget which produce different and complex patterns of activity, expenditure, value and outcome. The potential for error in setting fundholder budgets is considerable. It is therefore essential that all parties (General Practice Fundholders (GPFHs), RHAs, DHAs and Family Health Services Authorities (FHSAs)) sign up openly to the principle of *equity* or fairness in the distribution of available health care resources for a given population[2]. As fundholder hospital and community services allocations are top-sliced (deducted) from the DHA's allocation, this principle is clearly vital. Fundholding is not a device whereby additional money can be obtained for health services for a given population.

It is also important that attempts are made to reconcile the money spent by GPFHs against the available 'pot' of money. A typical DHA might spend 12% of its allocation on elective surgery (of which 30% falls outside the procedures currently included in the fund) and 11% on out-patient services. Thirty per cent of the available resource might be spent on emergency treatment and the remainder on community services (16%), maternity services (7%) and long-stay services (21%) including the elderly, mental illness and learning disabilities.

A relative increase in the slice of money spent on elective surgery will put pressure on the services used by fundholders for both emergency and long-stay care. It could also cause differential access to elective surgery between the patients of fundholding and non-fundholding practices, if the DHA is forced to reduce or restrain the amount spent on elective surgery to meet its other priorities; or if the volume of emergency work rises, as it has done in many parts of the country in the recent past.

If there is to be equal access to health care resources, then an equitable approach to allocating resources across all the elements of the fund must be applied. Variations in prescribing by individual GPs, for example, can lead to disproportionate amounts being allocated to different practices.

It is essential to consider not just the individual elements of the fund separately, but also the size of each fund in total, recognizing that there may well be some degree of interaction between expenditure on the different elements of the fund.

Joint agreement on priorities (such as the amount to be spent on emergency services) between all purchasers (fundholders and DHAs) is therefore important. The NHS has traditionally used spending on elective surgery as a balancing figure between other pressures. Whilst DHAs and GPFHs are to some extent in competition with each other as purchasers (and rightly so), that competition must be tempered by co-operation between them over issues of strategic importance to the population, if distortion and dislocation of the health-care system are to be avoided.

Such discussions on equity, priorities and methodology should be conducted in the summer/autumn, should precede the budget negotiation process with individual practices and should be considered by a representative group of GPs (fundholding and non-fundholding) and practice or fund managers. These crucial discussions should form the context and parameters for individual negotiations. They should also reassure DHAs over the fairness of the process and set the foundation for future dialogue over purchasing strategies.

# Hospital and community services

The hospital and community element of the fund is categorized into four parts:

- In-patients and day-cases.
- Out-patients.
- Diagnostic and direct access services.
- Community services.

For the in-patient and day-case element of the fund there is a prescribed list of procedures. Only the treatment of patients referred by a GP to a hospital consultant is deemed to be chargeable to the fund. Any emergency treatment of patients is excluded. In the case of out-patients, all out-patient referrals by a GP are chargeable regardless of whether any subsequent in-patient treatment is within the prescribed list. There are also specific exclusions for radiotherapy, chemotherapy, renal dialysis and attendances at genitourinary medicine (GUM) clinics.

All diagnostic tests are included in the scheme, with the specific exceptions of breast and cervical screening carried out under the national call and recall schemes, issue of hearing aids, and tests carried out by the Public Health Laboratory Service as a matter of public policy.

Direct access to paramedical services (the professions allied to medicine) forms part of the fund and includes those services to which GPs refer directly (or where consultants refer on following a GP referral). These services include physiotherapy, speech therapy and occupational therapy, but exclude local authority-supplied services and all maternity services other than pregnancy tests and antenatal blood tests not carried out as part of an out-patient appointment.

The fund for in-patients, day-cases and out-patients has so far been calculated by applying provider prices to the activity counted by GPs during the preparatory year. Prices supplied by provider units may be either by individual procedure or on a banding basis, where similar costed procedures are banded together for ease of calculation and comparison. The latter approach generally appears to result in a more acceptable outcome to all parties.

To avoid later disagreements as to the correctness of the activity count, a reconciliation of the activity must be undertaken between the fundholding practice and the relevant provider units where the service was carried out.

It is not always practicable to cover all provider units because of the volume of work, but the main units should be involved. This crucial validation process should cover not only the numerical accuracy of the data, but also the relevant category of patient, i.e. in-patient, day-case or out-patient.

As provider trusts become more sophisticated in their pricing for all parts of the service, there will inevitably be price changes which potentially affect the size of fund offers. It is most important to realize that any restructuring of costs by provider units, which increases or decreases GP fundholder prices, should also be reflected in prices actually charged by that unit to non-fundholding purchasers. These changes and the reasons for them have to be very carefully examined and explained to all parties.

In 1993–94 the fund was extended to include some of the community services previously purchased by DHAs, including health visiting, district nursing, dietetics, speech therapy and chiropody, as well as the mental health, learning disabilities and community services which were not previously included in the scheme. In the first year of the inclusion of these services the allocations were 'ring-fenced' to ensure that no disruption to provider units would take place. It must be anticipated that changes in service patterns will take place in 1994–95 and future years. Already problems of poor or no data and differing views on priorities make the need for concerted action obvious.

The way in which services are delivered in the future should have an impact on the size of the fund. During the first 3 years of fundholding there has been a considerable move by most provider units from in-patient to day-case surgery with a consequent reduction in cost. There is a strong case for reducing this part of the fund, but with an equally strong case for increasing the direct access services and community services to provide more resources for what is generally regarded as that part of the NHS which requires further investment.

There has been a tendency to negotiate funds on a roll-forward basis, only allowing for inflation increases and some small adjustments to reflect increased or decreased resources of the host DHAs, consequent upon their relative capitation positions. However, the principle of equity must embody not only the historic distribution of resources between the parties but also changes in medical practice. It is important that both aspects are considered by all stakeholders serving a local population on an annual basis.

# Prescribing

Prescribing budgets for GP fundholders, like target budgets for non-fundholders, are set within the context of a national strategy designed to promote good quality, rational and cost-effective prescribing by GPs. The overriding factor in determining the level of allocations to RHAs, FHSAs and ultimately to practices is the overall level of provision made by the Government for GP-prescribed drugs through the Public Expenditure Survey.

The exact mechanism for allocating budgets may vary from year to year as the strategy evolves, but the general principles that the RHA and FHSA will follow are:

- that there should be equity of access to available resources for the patients of both fundholding and non-fundholding practices; and

- that there should be firm downward pressure on historical levels of expenditure which appear to have no clinical justification.

Within these parameters, budgets for both fundholding and non-fundholding practices are set by reference to:

- previous years' allocations and spending patterns – currently there is a preference for relating budgets to previous allocations rather than to year-end out-turns of expenditure, to avoid discriminating against practices which have made efficiency savings in the past

- known changes in list size and in the number and distribution of high-cost patients; and, where possible

- local morbidity data.

In addition, there may be some movement towards a weighted capitation benchmark allocation. The NHS Executive is committed to the aim of a more objective and fairer distribution of resources based on a system of weighted capitation. While a national capitation formula remains to be agreed, it is common for FHSAs to calculate benchmark allocations on the basis of 'ASTRO-PUs' (Age, Sex, Temporary Resident Orientated Prescribing Units), a target allocation based on the practice's list size weighted for specific variables.

All budgets from the national budget downwards are calculated initially at net ingredient cost (NIC), and the aggregate total of all fundholders' allocations, non-fundholders' target budgets, and any contingency set aside for non-fundholders must be less than or equal to the total FHSA allocation.

The RHA will usually hold a contingency reserve for fundholders from which to make further allocations during the year in the event of any significant change in circumstances.

Finally, fundholders' allocations are converted from net ingredient cost to a cash equivalent to reflect the fact that the actual cost of drugs to the NHS is often discounted by drug companies following negotiations with the Government. This calculation is done using a factor (0.923 in 1994–95) specified by the NHS Executive. Because this factor varies from year to year, comparison between one year's allocation and another's should be made at NIC and not between cash allocations. It is this cash allocation which becomes the drugs element of the GP fundholder's annual budget.

## Practice staff

The practice staff element of the fund is intended to meet the cost of staff who are employed:

- to provide treatment to the patients of partners within the practice

- in connection with the management of the practice.

The fund should not be used to employ a medical practitioner nor should it be used to meet the cost of staff employed to manage the fund. Fund managers and other staff engaged in administering the fund are charged to the management allowance for which discrete funding is provided.

Staff budgets for fundholding practices are funded from cash-limited general medical services resources. As such they are calculated in the same way as staff budgets for non-fundholding practices, so as to ensure equity of resource distribution between fundholding and non-fundholding practices.

The practice staff scheme introduced in 1990 provided for the direct reimbursement of all or part of the expenses of employing staff, in accordance with an FHSA's local policy on the use of its cash-limited resources. Policies between FHSAs may vary in the light of local needs, but all will take account of service needs, the Authority's own cash allocation and the circumstances of the practice.

The budgeted amount will be no less than the cost of staff to whom transitional arrangements apply under paragraphs 52: 25–28 of the revised Statement of Fees and Allowances (SFAs). Practices may therefore expect to be funded at a level not less than the cost of such staff in post at 31 March 1990 providing:

- the practice has not increased the hours of employment

- there has been no increase in salary levels (other than reasonable salary increases)

- duties to be performed have not been modified significantly

- the percentage of salary costs reimbursed has not been increased.

Fundholding practices will be required, from their fees and allowances, to meet any difference between the directly reimbursed and actual costs, in respect of posts for which the practice has received direct reimbursement under the practice staff scheme immediately before joining the fundholding scheme.

Many FHSAs have adopted a capitation approach to setting practice staff budgets. Using practice lists as a basis some apply a weighting for age and sex whilst others consider weightings for factors such as branch surgeries or training partners. Target allocations calculated in this way are often used as a benchmark with a move from historical to capitation budgets taking several years to achieve.

The fund will be re-calculated each year to reflect changes (for example in practice list size and to meet the cost of agreed annual pay increases). Fundholding practices will not be expected to apply to the FHSA during the year for additional allocations. Some in-year adjustments to allocations may be agreed where significant changes take place within the practice (for example, a change in practice list size following the appointment of a new partner). Some FHSAs include an element to cover staff training costs though many retain a single FHSA budget for this purpose.

Fundholding practices may employ staff not covered by the practice staff element of the fund (for example counsellors). In situations where this has occurred as a consequence of transferring work from hospital or community services to the surgery, a practice may request a virement from the hospital element of the fund to supplement the staff element. Virement between all of the elements of the fund is also possible where new staff have been employed since the practice gained fundholding status.

A final budget offer will be made at the end of February each year either by the RHA or the FHSA acting on its behalf. Fundholders then have a full month to consider the offer before the start of the fund-holding year in April.

## Budget negotiation

The budget negotiating meetings with practices remain very individual. Although budgets calculated on a formula basis are of help in 'fixing' practices within a wide target band, a bespoke approach, using historic performance and local factors, is more appropriate[3]. Account has to be taken of provider prices in different areas as GPs tend to support their local providers and mainly use the market only when 'home' providers do not perform or for reasons of clinical quality or appropriateness.

The extent to which budget setting meetings are true negotiations is arguable. A typical agenda covers a review of the current year, a discussion on the business plans for the coming year and a detailed look at how the budget has been calculated. The review of the current year will consider current and projected activity and expenditure, contract and provider performance, waiting lists and a range of practice-specific issues.

The more years a practice has been in the scheme, the easier it is to identify trends; reviewing a GPFH in the first operational year with only 8 or 9 months' performance available is a challenge.

The relationship between the FHSA and GPFHs is under test during the negotiating process. The FHSA has recruited the practice into fund-holding, supported them during the preparatory year and acted as mentor and often friend. The move into budget setting and performance monitoring is an extension of the FHSA's role (delegated by the RHA), with the management, advising and policing roles co-existing and mutually understood. Each 'side', however, has considerable knowledge of each other; the practices have seen their budget offer and understand the methodology used.

The practice clearly recognizes it must stake its claim by commenting on its performance and likely year-end position, to which reliance on real numbers and the historical relationship of monthly expenditure to year-end position is an effective response. The meeting can then move forward into a review of GPFH's purchasing priorities and contracting intentions.

Planned developments are increasingly around moving secondary care into primary care settings, with GPs and their staff taking on an additional work-load. These plans are at the forefront of Government policy. It is at this point in the meeting that the need to retain an adequate budget to fund these developments is raised, often linked to the interface between the hospital, community, drugs and staff element of the fund.

When the budget setting stage is reached, the overall objective – setting a realistic budget whilst ensuring equity – and the methodology, calculations and considerations which have led to the bespoke budget are described and discussed. At this point practices tend to divide quite sharply. While virtually all practices accept the need to move towards equity of funding with their non-fundholding colleagues, their response to their own offer understandably varies. Most GPFHs put in a lot of hard work, clinically and managerially, to make fundholding a success in their practice.

There is a view in many practices that the NHS is good at penalizing success and rewarding failure and budget negotiations are often approached from this standpoint. Concentrating on jointly agreed objectives and values, rather than on the issues which divide the practice and the negotiator, moves the discussion to a conclusion and focuses on the year-round partnership between the fundholders and the FHSA. The negotiating team must be composed largely of managers known to the practices, where a working relationship already exists.

Adjournment in the face of impasse is a useful technique, followed by a letter briefly reiterating the arguments and making further suggestions for a 'safety net' review if budgets prove unreasonable. If absolutely necessary the RHA can provide an informal arbitration service, preventing the need for most cases of dispute to reach the NHS Executive.

In future the negotiating process should be characterized by substantially better knowledge and information, together with shared goals and priorities between DHAs and GPFHs, which can more logically link resources to objectives. Future budget negotiations will be a more sophisticated blend of the present formula and practice-sensitive approaches, which should change the budget setting negotiation from the rather dramatic event that it often is to an informed review of policy, operational targets and performance.

Agreement on funding could be comparatively routine within this scenario, but always with the flexibility of recognizing and responding to legitimate local features. Given all the difficulties, a system of checks and balances is essential to ensure mutual confidence and a fair result for the population served.

# References

1   Coulter A, Roland M and Wilkin D (1991) *GP Referrals to Hospital: A Guide for FHSAs*. Centre of Primary Care Research, University of Manchester.
2   Dixon J (1994) Can there be fair funding for fundholding practices? *British Medical Journal*, **308**: 772–75.
3   Freeman F (1994) Funding for fund holders: the 'feel free' factor. *Primary Health Care Management*, **4**(3): 12–14.

Contracts

*Tim Richardson and Bill Taylor*

## Introduction

One point must be made: there is no such thing as 'true' fundholding contracts. The Regulations for fundholding are the same as those for DHA/RHA purchaser/provider contracting. That is, contracts are based on mutual trust, entered into in good faith, cannot be the subject of litigation but, in the case of fundholding contracts, should be constructed to give either party rights to appeal to the relevant RHA for arbitration. In reality contract negotiations are generally conducted in the expectation that common sense and mutual professional respect will prevail and arbitration is not a factor.

## Forms of contract

There are four basic forms of fundholding contract:

- cost-per-case
- block
- non-attributable block
- cost and volume.

Variations in their application by different fundholders could achieve significantly different patient care standards with widely differing results for the practice. When considering which contract to pursue it would be sensible not to be over-influenced by other fundholders, who might have different aims, but to use wisely their experiences to achieve your own objectives. Local circumstances and different providers have varied effects on individual purchasers, and personalities may also become factors. Long-term relationships might be jeopardized and professional co-operation may be damaged in the process of agreeing contracts.

The first practices to start fundholding were often described as at the 'leading' edge of the profession; the epithet 'cutting' would have been more appropriate in some cases. Contracts were sometimes set up on a very aggressive over-detailed basis, with provider units cut to the financial bone. Conversely, some practices only specified simple block contracts because the provider insisted on operating 'ethically and sensitively', claiming the long-term professional bonds would be sundered if that trust were challenged. Experience suggests that neither extreme provides long-term advantage but each form of contract has its place.

The other general point to make about any contract is that it can be placed with NHS or independent sector health providers (which may be a hospital, clinic or individual consultant), provided they have been accredited for fundholding by the appropriate RHA or Family Health Services Authority (FHSA), which in practice means that they have to be allocated a provider code. There are general restrictions about referrals within a practice (the GP as provider) that are dealt with elsewhere in the section on the independent sector.

## Constraints and opportunities

### Earmarked budgets

Fundholding budgets may be allocated in such a way that certain contracting restrictions are placed on the practice.

- The nature of the contract for some services may be subject to central direction, non-attributable block contracts for community nursing services being typical.

- The sum to be spent on a given service may be subject to direction, that for 'people with learning difficulties' for example.

- The sum available under a given heading may be such that the range of choice of contractor is reduced to only one whose tariff can be afforded.

- The purchasing plan may have been drafted under different circumstances from those ultimately experienced and the budget formed on the basis of the plan may restrict opportunity.

- The budget bid may not have taken fully into account the number of patients already referred and who have yet to be seen. These patients may appear in the returns 'out of the blue' and can be an expensive surprise under certain forms of contract.

Whilst factors such as these may seem unhelpful they do present a challenge to make the best of the circumstances of the day. It is for the practice to use the variety of forms of contract creatively and overcome setbacks. Even where prescription seems total it is possible to use one year's contract to work towards a better framework for future years. This is particularly so for those services only recently introduced into the fundholding environment, where both purchaser and provider have much to do before reaching a satisfactory status quo.

## Waiting-list initiatives

Since fundholding started, various features of central direction have intervened to benefit patient care but have had unpredictable knock-on effects for fundholders. One such is waiting-list initiative money, for which hospitals have to bid each year. To the fundholding practice the application of waiting-list money has often seemed arbitrary and difficult to track. Hospitals tend to decide which cases are biddable without reference to the referring practice, and thereafter it can become difficult for the practice to know what is happening.

That is where the fundholding computer software could be used as computer 'siftware'. At the least it could inform the practice of patients who seemed to be getting near the time limit beyond which waiting-list money would be appropriate. But it can only inform if the data have been entered in the first place, so for contract monitoring purposes, back-loading referrals for a period of at least a year before starting fundholding allows these cases to be tracked. It then becomes a matter of negotiating with the hospital concerned to establish precisely what has happened and whether the practice should be liable for the cost or not. In the past this has not always proved to be a simple task and only vigilance when confronted with an invoice has avoided both the practice and the waiting-list initiative funding the same procedure. In such circumstances, it would be helpful if the appropriate proportion of the waiting-list allocation were devolved to the practice by the relevant DHA.

# The cost-per-case contract

## Characteristics

The cost-per-case contract allows the GP fundholder to offer an individual referral to any selected provider unit on a one-off basis, the referral being offered and accepted on its own merits and circumstances. It is this single factor which has attracted so many to become fundholders. It is becoming the most common form of contract for the costlier referral, because it gives the GP the greatest degree of control, especially over time and cost.

## Information

Cost-per-case referrals provide the greatest amount of information with each referral letter including nationally agreed minimum data about the patient. Likewise, on discharge the provider must include details of the procedure carried out on the patient, enabling the purchaser to ensure the procedure is correctly coded. This is important in monitoring costs, as providers have occasionally charged for a high-cost procedure when a low-cost one was later discovered to have been done. For example, a simple procedure done as part of an out-patient attendance might be charged as a day-case which is more expensive. It is also possible for a non-fundholding procedure to have been done but invoiced with an incorrect fundholding code, and this is simpler to verify with cost-per-case contracts.

## Quality

It is also necessary for the service specifications attached to the treatment to be established at the time of the referral. For example, following the initial out-patient referral, would further sanction be needed before a subsequent in-patient episode could be listed? Waiting times (for both out-patient and in-patient attendance), or diary dates offered at the time of the consultation, named consultant, discharge letters issued within an agreed time, use of day instead of in-patient surgery (a significant cost determinant) and location for the procedure are all factors which should enter into the contract negotiation. Additionally there is the question of whether the costs include all tests and investigations, or whether benefit would be derived if some or all were done by the GP in advance. Naturally, it would be a financial waste and inconvenient to the patient if they were done twice.

All of these elements could be implied in the contract but it is preferable for them to be agreed and spelt out from the start. They then rapidly become second nature to the practice staff placing the referral and form part of the quality issues agreed between practice and provider under which individual referrals are made.

## Administration

With a cost-per-case contract the practice has a greater administrative load. For each referral there is more detail in the referral procedure and the monitoring as it proceeds from expected date of action to notified date of action and thence to invoice. The invoicing process is also more cumbersome. Consequently, cost-per-case should be used only when necessary, i.e. for high-cost low-volume activities, especially surgical procedures.

Payment becomes due within 2–3 weeks of presentation of invoice and it can be difficult to establish within that time whether the invoice is valid. For example, if a provider presents at month end a schedule of a hundred episodes many of them may have to be challenged, with practice staff spending many hours sorting this out. As, later, audit is to be satisfied then every referral invoiced separately must be verified and authorized, but if an individual referral costs only £10 (i.e. a simple pathology test) but has to be clarified, overload and frustration would be inevitable. Problems arise when patients of other practices, temporary residents and those who have self-referred, all get invoiced together with genuine referrals.

Nevertheless, if the practice wants to keep track of all its individual referrals for each named patient, this is the type of contract to go for.

## Cost

Usually, the provider has a tariff for each procedure, so the financial exposure should be established in advance. In the first 2 years of fund-holding many providers' finance departments experienced great difficulty in coping with cost-per-case contracts, being unable to identify procedures performed or their individual cost. This no longer applies and systems have been tightened up to give adequate cost/procedure data for most referrals.

Where there is no tariff, as might be with some regional specialties for procedures that are rarely performed, the provider could charge on a daily rate and the total cost may come as a shock after discharge. This arrangement should be avoided if at all possible.

Where some practices fall short is in failing to update progress of the episode, preferring to wait for the invoice, before entering details of the procedure and its cost. This might mean less administration, with one less input required for each episode but it negates what the fundholding software system intends, which is accurate cash-flow forecasting. Unless accrued costs of started cases are taken into account, fundholders will never be sure of their year-end position, and contract monitoring becomes a lottery. In particular, some cardiothoracic procedures cost so much that to ignore them until invoiced will be financially damaging.

Total cost is also important in the nature of the cost limit per patient per year. When a patient reaches the limit in any year, all referrals for that patient should be taken into account for full credit to be taken. The extra work has to be balanced against the financial benefit. For example, for every pathology cost to be included would require cost-per-case contracts for each request and a large volume of extra work for the few patients exceeding the limit.

# The block contract

## Characteristics

When fundholding started in 1991 the accepted wisdom was that the block contract was likely to be extensively used, especially whilst experience was built up. It is a contract where the purchasing practice guarantees a sum of money for a specified time to cover a defined range of procedures, such as all out-patient referrals, or all pathology requests. Most commonly it covers a 12-month period. It is by definition a contract without limit of volume so the purchaser can refer as many, or as few, as required and the provider may, or may not, deal with all or some of these during the period of the contract.

It puts no pressure on the provider, who receives the agreed sum whether or not the expected volume is reached. But it does give the provider a guaranteed income against which the range of services can be provided, whereas the cost-per-case contract guarantees only the cost of that case. If every provider had to rely only on cost-per-case income, life would be very uncertain. Thus the block contract is attractive to providers and forms the basis of many district contracts. As is well known, it is common for providers to over-perform on district block contracts during the early part of the year, often to the detriment of fundholder referrals, with the effect that fundholders are left worrying whether their own contracts are likely to be fulfilled by the year-end. By then it can be too late to make other arrangements. This is a manifestation of one difficulty of block contracts, namely that their very flexibility can bring uncertainty to the purchaser.

## Information

Block contracts may contain clauses giving the expected volume and hence notional cost of individual referrals but they can only be indicative, and are not volume-dependent.

The practice is able to use block contracts to identify the individual patient episode and the general nature of the referral, specialty etc., but is not able to guarantee patient-specific feedback from the provider, except so far as individual consultant discharge letters may identify detail. For example, it would be unusual to know of any procedure performed as part of an out-patient attendance. In one sense it is not important, in that if the practice were paying a lump sum the content of the episode would not affect overall cost, but it could be important for the patient care plan and accurate activity analysis. Thus block contracts are useful where routine functions are concerned and little detail is required. They are particularly useful for high-turnover low-cost activity such as pathology contracts.

The disadvantages of block contracts to the practice lie in the lack of detailed feedback in relation to the individual patient, inflexibility in the light of changes in referral patterns, absence of any guarantee that the provider performance will match that expected and difficulty in assessing quality standards.

## Quality

So far as the practice is concerned, the benefits of block contracts are confined to administration and finance whereby there is less to do to manage them, and greater fund control.

The block contract skates over many quality issues, particularly those relating to individual patient episodes. It would be reasonable to set out general standards such as availability of walk-in facilities for tests, waiting time in out-patients and expected response time for consultant letters but monitoring often has to rely on surveys and other indirect or indicative measures rather than objective measurement.

## Administration

The block contract requires less administration by the practice because it is in simple terms. Where this becomes important is in setting follow-on contracts. A practice ought to be aware of the progress of its block contracts in enough detail to know if value for money is being obtained. In the case of pathology contracts, for example, if all test requests are given equal weight the balance between one group and another can be impossible to determine and at year-end the chance of splitting the data, and hence the contract, between groups is lost. Contracting is not a static function and progress is made in proportion to the detailed knowledge available to the purchaser. The more that is known, the more that can be achieved. Practices need to monitor as much detail of block contracts as can be managed within their own computer and organizational capacity, which is an apparent contradiction to expectations of simplicity.

## Cost

Some practices base their out-patient block contracts on the expected number of new referrals. It would be simpler, although more work, to anticipate every attendance (new and follow-up) and to base the contract on that total, provided the notional cost per attendance can be weighted for the extra costs of each new referral. This, however, puts no pressure on the provider to reduce follow-up ratios.

Cost will not be itemized in a block contract invoice, the practice paying a lump sum each month, or at other agreed intervals, reaching the agreed total by year-end. Hence a block contract would be attractive to the practice when high volume and/or low individual referral cost were involved. Typically, this would apply to general out-patient, community, pathology and radiology (plain film) contracts and possibly to chiropody or physiotherapy.

When the work-load does not match the expected volume, one side or the other gains and the only redress is for any following contract to be re-priced accordingly. To guard against under- or over-performance a shorter-term contract, such as for 3 or 6 months, is recommended so that the remainder of the year can be covered more realistically. This could result in a provider being unable to establish the optimum level of service without longer-term income guarantees, but shorter-term block contracts do protect the purchaser.

It should be possible to specify that a block contract is amended or renegotiated if volume turns out greater or less than a percentage different from that intended, but this would make for uncertain financial planning and is where cost and volume contracts become relevant, to be discussed later.

## Variations on the block contract

For a contract with all services provided by a given provider at his own site the contract conditions could be straightforward and consistent between purchasers. Any variations would be a measure of the persistency and charm of the negotiators! This does not stop providers putting attractive quality terms into an out-patient contract so as to be more certain of attracting the higher-cost in-patient procedures that follow. That is where outreach services become important, although these could be appropriate in any form of contract.

## Outreach services

If a practice wishes to participate more directly in the services given under any contract this introduces a more negotiable situation. Most commonly, if a practice sought outreach clinics at the surgery it could expect reimbursement for use of premises, staff and equipment. Where the partners provide clinical support that too could be funded. In consequence a significant sum could be due to the practice. Whether the partners decided to negotiate the total contract price downward or to seek a specific cost reimbursement would depend upon the practice's financial circumstances, and advice should be sought before commitment. The treatment of income would be different in these two cases, with the former accruing as savings whereas the latter could be an up-front payment but would then come directly into the practice income stream and be taxable. The latter, however, is certain; the former (i.e. the savings) is always open to interference by RHA or FHSA.

Outreach services need not be constrained within block contracts and the same principle would apply to other contracts. If day or minor surgery beyond that covered by general medical services (GMS) were to be done at the surgery, whether by a consultant or by consultant and GP working together, this could be either as an extension of a hospital contract or as a separate contract in its own right. In the latter case there would be complications regarding the provider designation. The former arrangement is the simpler to set up, to maintain and to monitor.

# The non-attributable block contract

## Characteristics

The non-attributable block contract allows the placement of a nominal contract at a notional sum, which could be as low as £1, for a specified service delivered in an unrecorded manner. It has been likened to the old £1 premium bond in that you could strike the jackpot but the chances of so doing were infinitesimal. It was introduced to cover community nursing contracts where in 1992–93 providers were unable to meet any reasonable data requirement because caseload data had not been recorded in a suitable form. It is available to fundholders as a contract of choice for other services too.

The non-attributable block contract is suited to the situation where a contract is needed but there is no requirement for any detail, or there is no possibility of providing any detail. Circumstances when this could happen would be in, say, a physiotherapy contract where the practice decided it only needed the most basic form of contract requiring the physiotherapist to be available on site for any referred cases, for a sum of money to be allocated for an unspecified range and number of procedures.

Non-attribution does not imply lack of influence over the terms of the contract. For example, in a non-attributable community nursing contract it would be reasonable to:

- seek some control over day-to-day management costs of community staff and administrative back-up

- specify the staff by name

- know what cover was to be provided for leave, sickness etc.

- know how much time was to be devoted to training and administration

- require the attendance of the staff at primary health care meetings.

It would also be reasonable to seek surgery-based services rather than locality based, if that were considered clinically preferable and adequate space was available.

This type of contract would save recording time, would require a provider to undertake a service and would specify the user of that service. It would also allow a breathing space whilst practice and provider developed more understanding of the nature of the service required. It is frequently used when the budget allocation is known to be unrealistic but, nevertheless, it is essential to be assured of a service. Inevitably, it is necessary where the fundholder has an unrealistically low budget allocation and the DHA keeps the balance. Then it is necessary for both DHA and fundholder to use the same provider unit which thus receives the same overall funding.

What it would not do would be to provide any information about the level or quality of service provided. By definition this would be absent. If more were required then another form of contract should be sought. However, crude activity data can be sought and should be available, allowing a more detailed budget application the following year – and more specific future contracts.

# The cost and volume contract

## Characteristics

The cost and volume contract was envisaged as a compromise between the cost-per-case and block in that it contains a modicum of both and was thought to avoid some of their problems. In principle it allows the bulk of the work to be covered under block arrangements with a selective element on top costed individually. Some practices favour this model because they see it as offering more flexibility when workload is uncertain; others see it as offering only the worst of both types. Many contracts use the term block for what are in reality cost and volume contracts, because they have specific volume limits included.

A cost and volume contract works by setting the volume limit for the block element and then counting down until this total is reached, after which a cost-per-case charge is made. Some providers may have difficulty in coping with this form of contract – their computer software may go into spasm when trying to set limits – so check beforehand that the software can cope.

## Information

In 1991 it was anticipated that most in-patient referrals would be on a cost and volume basis but the trend has been towards cost-per-case. The reason for this has been evident in the lack of complete control over detail in cost and volume, together with the fact that it would demand nearly as much work in the practice without the maximum return available with cost-per-case. When considering a cost and volume contract it would also be worth while to take into account the provider's information flow as it could be restricted.

Information flow in most providers is now geared to cost-per-case contracts and cost and volume contracts would best be used if a specified number of procedures were to be purchased in a package. By this means the monitoring process would be simplified and could be effective.

## Quality

As has been suggested, the cost and volume contract offers both advantages and disadvantages over the other two main types of contract and in quality terms has no unique features to offer that would set it apart from them. The provider could be expected to reach the same general quality standards as for other types of contract.

## Administration

The benefit to a practice in choosing cost and volume would be that it could smooth out the variability inherent in block without requiring all the detail of cost-per-case. It means that the bulk of the commitment would be known and could be planned for. It would give both purchaser and provider an incentive lacking in block contracts.

## Cost

A typical cost and volume contract might specify a maximum number of procedures to be covered beyond which any additions would be at a nominated individual cost, which might be at marginal cost or at some other adjusted rate. Alternatively, if the specified throughput was not achieved then a reduced cost would be accepted.

There are also special forms of this type of contract whereby a zero volume is assumed for the block contract so that a single sum can be entered against one referral as if it were a block contract. This offers a convenient financial ploy on occasion when a lump sum payment may be required for more than one episode.

# Value for money

## The nature of the contract

Value for money is a term that can be much abused. Providers and purchasers may have very different attitudes to it and a fundholding contract has to be an agreement between a willing buyer and a willing seller. Both parties have to see the content as satisfying their basic financial requirements, protecting their professional interests and offering a high or higher standard of care to the patient. The location, personnel, equipment, training and management contribute to value for money. In the current climate, with many hospitals apparently under threat of loss of business and possible closure, value for money may be in danger of compromise in the interest of survival. It is in this context that there is value in the non-legalistic nature of fundholding contracts, because both parties can negotiate a satisfactory standard of performance without undermining the fundamental nature of the relationship.

## The balance between quality and cash

Measurement of value for money can be difficult and to date it has been common for quality issues to be less prominent than cash in contract monitoring. Cash has been king to date, largely because providers have been struggling to get on top of the necessary control mechanisms and they have not been amenable to challenges on either quality or value for money.

## Payment issues

The nature of the contract is that of timeliness and accuracy coupled with high-quality performance. It is probably worth while to set out in the contract certain limits beyond which payment becomes withheld, temporarily or permanently. It has been known for a service or procedure to be invoiced more than a year after it has been performed. It is unreasonable to expect such an invoice to be honoured and the contract should set a time limit for payment. This has now been agreed nationally as 6 weeks. Similarly, a practice cannot be expected continually to be correcting invoices when found in error, and there is sense in specifying a limit to this debilitating activity.

On the other hand, it is unreasonable to expect a provider to make radical changes to a service in mid-contract, such as if the referral rate fails to reach expectations in a block contract. One possible approach would be to reach a mutual understanding that could apply adjustments in the following year, or to use 6-month contracts, or even a 9-month block followed by a final 'adjusted' 3-month period.

## Best value for money

In contracting terms, there is no single 'best value for money' overall. Each form of contract has benefits and disadvantages in some circumstances and the best fit is likely to be found after very careful assessment of all the factors. Taking one year with another, it does not necessarily follow that in successive years the same form of contract is best for the same service, because where there is change in the need, so also could there be a need for a change.

In general, there is little doubt that a cost-per-case contract for an in-patient procedure is the most effective for the GP and the patient: it puts the provider under the greatest constraint and defines the limit of the practice's exposure but it does not necessarily incur the lowest cost for any given procedure. It is a less attractive form for high-volume, low-cost procedures because of the changing balance between workload and benefit. Some practices do use this form for every hospital procedure and benefit from the greater control and information, deeming it worthwhile to incur the extra work-load.

The block contract is best used for high-volume, low-cost work when lack of detail and of individual control is tolerable. It can be very effective where a wide variety of referrals is anticipated and cost averaging is desired, for it limits the total cost outlay. Quality controls are more limited, as stated earlier.

The non-attributable block contract is best regarded as a temporary expedient pending the opportunity to specify more accurately what is required. The practice must be able to provide a better service for the patient when it has more information and control than this type offers.

The cost and volume contract offers a half-way house, being neither the best nor the worst in most circumstances. It offers some flexibility so is best regarded as a useful interim solution where there is uncertainty. It can be successfully used when purchasing a package of procedures for a marginal cost, particularly towards the end of a year when capacity may become available at short notice.

## Monitoring

Once fundholding starts, contract monitoring in-year is essential. It is no good leaving it until at or near year-end; for one thing there is need for knowledge so as to negotiate contracts for year two. There are monthly, quarterly and half-yearly tasks to be done, and the computer software offers considerable scope for automatic reporting. It would be easy to get indigestion and selection is important. That is where perspective is vital: contracts cover widely differing costs, volumes and complexity of case-load. It is up to each practice to assess each contract's clinical, financial and managerial aspects so that only the elements important to that practice are subject to frequent monitoring. Others will be interested, such as the FHSA and RHA, but their requirements may not tally with those of the practice, even though they require much effort before being satisfied. The role of the managing partner and careful specification of tasks between partner and managers is crucial to a successful outcome.

Contracting is an art, not a science. There is an innumerable variety of successful contracts. It is for each practice to discover what suits it best.

8    The Role of the FHSA or Health
        Commission

*Clive Parr*

Some Regions have decided to delegate almost total responsibility for
GP fundholding issues to Family Health Services Authorities (FHSAs) or
Health Commissions (HCs). Others have retained a fairly tight central
grip on fundholding and its development. Most Regions and FHSAs/HCs
have issued guidance to fundholders about their local working relationships. Therefore, potential fundholders should make a point of contacting their FHSA/HC at an early date to obtain this local guidance.


## Planning cycle

Around the turn of each year FHSAs/HCs will write to medical practices
in their areas seeking expressions of interest about entering the next
wave of fundholding commencing the following April. Because it is
possible for practices to join together to form a fundholding consortium,
or to join a multifund, all practices will usually be contacted. There is, of
course, nothing to preclude practices contacting FHSAs/HCs at any stage
about their interest in fundholding and seeking their assistance in taking
an application forward. FHSAs/HCs may also be able to suggest 'suitable
partners' for practices who do not qualify in their own right.
   Table 8.1 is a typical planning overview for a practice entering the
preparatory year of fundholding. Table 8.2 shows a typical planning
cycle for practices already within the fundholding scheme. It is important
that the dates agreed with the FHSA/HC as part of the planning cycle for
submission of the various reports and other information are adhered to.
What at first sight can seem a fairly formidable process in terms of
the collection of activity data and the submission of reports, business
plans and quarterly monitoring information will be fully explained to
practices as part of a continuing programme of training activity for both

**Table 8.1** Preparatory year of fundholding

| | |
|---|---|
| April | Discussion with FHSA/HC on computer hardware/software leading to a bid for funding.<br>Practice starts collecting data. |
| May | Training of practice staff involved in fundholding commences.<br>Data collection continues. |
| June | Regional office will confirm activity data requirements. |
| July | |
| August | Discussions with providers to agree activity levels for budget setting purposes. |
| September | FHSA/HC agree base activity levels with fundholders. |
| October | Proposed major changes in contracts for the following year to be notified to FHSA/HC.<br>Budget meetings with FHSA/HC. |
| November | FHSA/HC discuss staff/drug budgets with GP fundholders.<br>Provider prices due. |
| December | |
| January | FHSA/HC agree budgets at following year's prices.<br>Staff and budgets also formally agreed with FHSA/HC. |
| February | FHSA/HC corporate contract communicated to GP fundholders who will take note of this when producing business plans.<br>Business plan for the first year of fundholding sent to FHSA/HC. |
| March | Green light to GP fundholding. |

**Table 8.2** GP fundholding – annual planning overview

| | |
|---|---|
| January | Budget allocations to GPFHs:<br>FHSA/HC workshop:<br>  • Business planning<br>  • Community care<br>  • Contracting |
| February | FHSA/HC communicate corporate contract and public health reports to GPFHs who will take note of these when producing business plans. |
| March | FHSA/HC submit aggregate of business plans to Regional Office.<br>End of financial year. |
| April | Start of financial year. |
| May | Monthly monitoring report. |
| June | Activity data requirements confirmed to GPFHs/providers for next financial year.<br>End quarter one.<br>Monthly monitoring report. |
| July | Monthly monitoring report.<br>Quarterly monitoring report. |
| August | Practices begin to agree activity levels with providers.<br>Monthly monitoring report. |
| September | FHSA/HC negotiate staff/drugs budget.<br>End of quarter two.<br>Monthly monitoring report. |
| October | Activity levels confirmed.<br>GPFHs communicate major purchasing changes to FHSA/HC.<br>Monthly monitoring report.<br>Quarterly monitoring report. |
| November | Provider prices due.<br>Monthly monitoring report. |
| December | Budget meetings with FHSA/HC.<br>End of quarter three.<br>Monthly monitoring report. |
| January | Budget allocations to GPFHs.<br>Monthly monitoring report.<br>Quarterly monitoring report. |
| February | Communication of following year's corporate contract and public health reports to GPFHs from FHSA/HC.<br>Deadline for business plans.<br>Monthly monitoring report. |
| March | FHSA/HC submit aggregate business plans to Regional Office.<br>Monthly monitoring report.<br>End of financial year. |
| April | Monthly monitoring report. |

established fundholding practices and those wishing to enter the scheme. These training events will be arranged by the FHSA/HC or the Regional Office.

## Accountability

To the unenlightened, GP fundholders are 'the wild cards in the pack', seemingly accountable to no one but themselves. The reality of course is very different.

Fundholding is governed by statute – the NHS (Fundholding Practices) Regulations 1993. A copy of these Regulations should be available in every fundholding practice. The Regulations cover recognition and the renunciation of the recognition of fundholders, appeals to the Secretary of State against refusal of recognition or the removal of recognition. In short, there are regulations governing the setting of budgets, a requirement not to overspend as well as regulations governing the use to which budgets and savings can be put.

All fundholding accounts held by practices and FHSA/HCs are subject to audit by the Audit Commission on an annual basis. Staff from the Audit Commission are keen to see that proper use has been made of the funds allocated. In addition, most FHSA/HCs have also made arrangements for their own internal auditors to carry out audit work with fundholders. The FHSA/HC will liaise with practices, internal and Audit Commission auditors about the precise arrangements and to avoid overlap.

Business and purchasing plans produced by the fundholders are also required to be approved by FHSA/HCs. Corporate contracts produced by Authorities reflecting their own business plans for the year are usually also made available to fundholders, as are the reports of the local Directors of Public Health. Fundholders are expected to take account of both local and national issues in preparing their business and purchasing plans and the availability of corporate contracts and the reports of the Directors of Public Health will enable them to do so.

Built into the planning cycle is a series of monthly and quarterly monitoring reports. These reports cover both financial matters and waiting-list information. The information is required so that FHSA/HCs can monitor progress and address problems as they arise. Monitoring arrangements are dealt with in more detail below.

A number of FHSA/HCs have also established a system of performance review for general practices in their areas, including of course fundholders. In my own area an annual review is held with every practice in the county using a computer-based management information system to bring together a comprehensive range of information held by the FHSA about the practice concerned. Details of medical and support staff, surgery arrangements, an age profile of the patients, immunization and cervical cytology screening performance, prescribing information and costs, referral patterns, socio-economic information about patients in the practice area, health promotion and minor surgery activity are all included. In addition the practice annual report is used as a resource document at the review. If the practice is a fundholder a separate section is added to the review process to cover fundholding during the year.

Fundholders are in precisely the same position for clinical accountability as non-fundholders. Medical audit is now being successfully developed in most parts of the country. This will often involve practices in producing protocols, for example, dealing with the treatment of asthmatics and diabetics within the practice and perhaps also a practice prescribing formulary.

Fundholding recognition between an Authority and a practice has to be renewed annually as part of the budget negotiations. This presents an opportunity for all concerned to reflect on the desirability of continuing in the scheme. Practices wishing to withdraw may only do so on the 31 March following the sending of notice to the RHA. Notice must be given by no later than the end of February.

There are a wide range of mechanisms available to FHSA/HCs and Regions to hold fundholders to account. The NHS Authorities wish to work constructively with fundholders, and it will rarely be the case that a fundholding practice has to be removed from the scheme. It is nevertheless worth bearing in mind that this sanction is open to an RHA or on appeal to the Secretary of State and has already been used in a small number of cases.

## Business and purchasing plans

Some FHSAs/HCs treat these two topics separately. In my own area we feel they are so intrinsically linked that we prefer to deal with them together. The plan is an accepted means of communicating changes in delivery of service and purchasing intentions. In it, practices set out details of their mission as a practice, their aims and objectives, purchasing intentions and a note of any savings they intend to try to make. The Plan also requires some input in terms of health needs assessment to link with the FHSAs/HCs corporate contract and the challenging targets of the Government's *Health of the Nation* document. The Directors of Public Health for each district are responsible for communicating local health needs to practices so that all GPs and primary health care teams can have an opportunity to address these local health priorities. Practices will find the Annual Report of their Director of Public Health invaluable in addressing local health needs as part of the planning process.

The importance of business planning cannot be overestimated in the light of the growing numbers of fundholding practices and the likelihood of increasing numbers and types of service falling within the scope of the fund. The range of information required within the plan will be reviewed annually by Authorities as part of the rolling planning process and is designed to have a dual function. Units and health care providers will benefit in that they will be able to plan services more effectively and GP fundholders will themselves be in a position to monitor their progress on a year on year basis.

The FHSA/HC also uses the plan to monitor the progress of fund-holders. The mid-year review of the process exists not only to provide support to practices but also to establish performance against the following criteria:

- financial monitoring requirements
- Patient's Charter waiting list and quality standards
- FHSA corporate contract standards
- contract monitoring arrangements.

It is difficult to be precise about what a business and purchasing plan might look like but the following headings may be found a helpful lead into the subject.

## Mission statement

For example, a commitment to maintain a high standard of family medicine to the mutual satisfaction of patients, doctors and staff.

## Conducting an analysis of the practice's strengths and weaknesses

This is commonly called a SWOT analysis and will identify *s*trengths, *w*eaknesses, *o*pportunities and *t*hreats. The subject will usually be dealt with at a training workshop when the practice will be encouraged to identify its strengths and weaknesses and to plan for the future.

## Aims and objectives

The aims and objectives of the practice might cover the planned use of the management allowance; planned use of the computer allowance; how data are to be collected and by whom; an insight into likely planned changes in purchasing intentions; a review of the objectives set out in the previous year; a reflection of the practice's population health needs drawn from the report of the Director of Public Health; proposed use of planned savings; and training issues and quality objectives, including audit schemes. It is always worth remembering the five golden rules for objective setting. Objectives should be:

- achievable
- specific
- measurable (wherever possible)
- timed
- not too many.

Purchasing intentions might include a commitment to purchase as efficiently as possible whilst aiming to further reduce waiting lists. This may mean assessing specialties as to their ability to provide the necessary service and may result in a need to identify providers who may be able to supply extra throughput. No doubt most practices will also wish to address the continuing trend and encouragement towards day-case surgery. One of our practices has set itself these two targets:

- sixty per cent of all surgery will be carried out on a day-case basis
- eighty per cent of all surgery will be minimally invasive.

For out-patients, practices will wish to look at contracting for fixed achievable attendance levels whilst looking at ways of reducing follow-up attendances. It may also be appropriate to assess which services might more appropriately be provided within the practice. One of our practices has set itself the following target: 40% of out-patient consultations will take place outside a district general hospital.

A view will also need to be taken on the availability of direct access tests and therapy. Will these continue to be purchased from the same provider or should the service be changed in some way?

Similar considerations will apply to the community nursing services. Current rules require practices to contract with an NHS provider of these services. Are the existing services adequate and is there a possibility of moving community services to another NHS provider?

## Savings/spending plans

At the end of the financial year practices may find that they have not spent all of their budget. Indeed, because of the changes in the way certain services have been provided fundholders may have a planned underspend which they can use for the benefit of patients. An indication of any planned savings should form part of the business plan. Once the practice's fundholding account has been audited a savings plan can be prepared and submitted to the FHSA/HC. The funds determined as savings may be used to pay for additional staff or hospital services, providing additional medical equipment or improving facilities for patients.

The savings plan must demonstrate the cost and service delivery parameters of any intended purchase so that the FHSA/HC can reach an informed decision as to whether to grant approval. The net amount of year-end savings is defined as the amount by which the total practice fund, that is combined hospital community health services, drugs and practice staff elements, exceeds total expenditure for that year. Any material items that have come to light during the audit process that affect the level of declared savings must be a first call on them – for example, the year-end creditors will be carried forward to the following year. Where the assessment of year-end creditors carried forward turns out to be too low the amount shown in the savings account will, accordingly, be too high. If this is the case fundholders should identify overstated savings to meet the excess of the invoiced amounts over the assessed amount. As long as the assessment of creditors is prudent and based on the best information available the need to use savings in this way will be very small.

There is currently no fixed national policy governing the break-down of savings in percentage terms. Most FHSAs/HCs would expect, however, to see a large proportion of any savings made redirected towards patient services and Patient's Charter initiatives. Some examples of the use of savings appearing regularly in savings plans are:

- purchase of extra operations to reduce waiting lists
- purchase of in-house services such as physiotherapy, chiropody and counselling
- purchase of equipment to improve minor surgery
- purchase of additional training courses for staff
- purchase of hospital consultants' time to run out-patient clinics in the surgery.

The fundholding regulations also permit the improvement of the structure of the practice premises or the purchase of furniture and furnishings for the premises.

# Reports to the FHSA and monitoring

As indicated earlier, FHSA/HCs have all produced their own local systems for monitoring and reporting arrangements. They can, however, be divided broadly into two distinct headings: financial monitoring and monitoring against Patient's Charter quality standards and local health needs assessment issues.

Table 8.3 indicates the statements, schedules and reports that will be required by the FHSA/HC and their date of submission. These reports are all generated by the approved fundholding software.

Patient's Charter quality standards information will also be collected quarterly by the FHSA/HC. The in-patient requirement will be to see that no patients wait more than 12 months before in-patient or day-case admission and that all out-patients receive their first appointment within 12 weeks (Figure 8.1). Information will also be collected from each practice on a quarterly basis about the performance of provider units the practice has contracted with for services.

Finally, from April 1994 practices will be required to produce monthly purchasing plan information. This will be collected by FHSAs/HCs and Regional Offices to assist strategic planning and ensure effective monitoring of market risk (Figure 8.2).

**Table 8.3** Statements, schedules and reports required by the FHSA/HC

| Report number | | Report title | Deadline |
|---|---|---|---|
| Statement | 1 | Fund income & expenditure | Three weeks from |
| | 2 | Savings account | the end of the |
| | 3 | Balance sheet | month to which |
| | 5 | Fund cash analysis | they relate. |
| | | | |
| Schedule | 1 | Hospital services expenditure report | Three weeks from |
| | 2 | Analysis of proportion of staff costs | the end of the |
| | 6 | FHSA/HC account | month to which |
| | 12 | Analysis of community nursing costs | they relate. |
| | | | |
| Report | 3 | Hospital service accruals | Three weeks from |
| | 4 | Claim for treatment costs over £6,000 | the end of the |
| | 8 | Analysis of treatment by summary | month to which |
| | | | they relate. |

The following supplementary information is also required monthly.

- Reasons for under/over-expenditure:
  - hospital services
  - drugs
  - staff.
- Causes of delay in producing statements.
- Known errors/omissions from the accounts.
- Planned year-end position.
- Estimated year-end position for hospital services based on local knowledge.

Information required quarterly should reach the FHSA by the end of the month following the quarter end.

Information required monthly should reach the FHSA by the third week of the month following the month in question.

Hereford and Worcester FHSA

Waiting Time Analysis

Practice Name:　　　　　　　　Month of:

Numbers on Waiting List by Months Waiting

**Part 1 Inpatients**

| Main Specialty | 0<3 | 3<6 | 6<9 | 9<12 | 12<15 | 15<18 | 18<21 | 21<24 | 24+ | Total |
|---|---|---|---|---|---|---|---|---|---|---|
| General Surgery | | | | | | | | | | |
| Urology | | | | | | | | | | |
| Orthopaedics | | | | | | | | | | |
| ENT | | | | | | | | | | |
| Ophthalmology | | | | | | | | | | |
| Gynaecology | | | | | | | | | | |
| Cardiothoracic | | | | | | | | | | |
| Total | | | | | | | | | | |

**Part 2 Day Cases**

| Main Specialty | 0<3 | 3<6 | 6<9 | 9<12 | 12<15 | 15<18 | 18<21 | 21<24 | 24+ | Total |
|---|---|---|---|---|---|---|---|---|---|---|
| General Surgery | | | | | | | | | | |
| Urology | | | | | | | | | | |
| Orthopaedics | | | | | | | | | | |
| ENT | | | | | | | | | | |
| Ophthalmology | | | | | | | | | | |
| Gynaecology | | | | | | | | | | |
| Cardiothoracic | | | | | | | | | | |
| Total | | | | | | | | | | |

**Figure 8.1** Example of waiting-time analysis form

Hereford and Worcester FHSA

Waiting Time Analysis

Practice Name:                    Month of:

Numbers on Waiting List by Months Waiting

**Part 1 Outpatients**

| Main Specialty | 0<3 | 3<6 | 6<9 | 9<12 | 12<15 | 15<18 | 18<21 | 21<24 | 24+ | Total |
|---|---|---|---|---|---|---|---|---|---|---|
| Paediatrics | | | | | | | | | | |
| Geriatrics | | | | | | | | | | |
| Other Medical | | | | | | | | | | |
| Orthopaedics | | | | | | | | | | |
| ENT | | | | | | | | | | |
| Ophthalmology | | | | | | | | | | |
| Gynaecology | | | | | | | | | | |
| Other Surgery | | | | | | | | | | |
| Mental Health | | | | | | | | | | |
| Other Specialties | | | | | | | | | | |
| Total | | | | | | | | | | |

Completed By:                    Tel No:

**Figure 8.1** *cont.*

Hereford and Worcester FHSA

Activity Purchased by GP Fundholders 1993/94

Practice Name: _____   Month of: _____

| | Month ACTUAL | YEAR TO DATE | | 1993/94 FORECAST OUTTURN | 1993/94 PLAN |
| | | ACTUAL | PLAN | | |
| | A | B | C | D | E |
|---|---|---|---|---|---|
| **GENERAL & ACUTE (including geriatrics) FINISHED CONSULTANT EPISODES (FCE's)** | | | | | |
| 1 Ordinary Elective Admissions | | | | | |
| 2 Day Cases | | | | | |
| | | | | | |
| **OUTPATIENT ATTENDANCES** | | | | | |
| 3 General and Acute | | | | | |
| 4 Other (Mental Health etc.) | | | | | |
| | | | | | |
| **COMMUNITY CARE CONTACTS** | | | | | |
| 5 Community and Paramedical Contacts | | | | | |

COMPLETED BY: _____        TEL. NO: _____

**Figure 8.2** Monthly purchasing-plan information forms

Hereford and Worcester FHSA

Practice Name:                    Month of:

| GPFH PURCHASING PLANS | 1992/93 OUTTURN £000 A | 1993/94 PLAN £000 B | 1993/94 FORECAST OUTTURN £000 C | PLAN Vs FORECAST OUTTURN (B – C) £000 D | Month Plan Profile £000 E | Cumulative Expenditure £000 F | Profile vs Actual (E – F) £000 G |
|---|---|---|---|---|---|---|---|
| SECTION A | | | | | | | |
| 1. Resources available | | | | | | | |
| 1.1 Allocation available for purchasing patient services | | | | | | | |
| 1.2 Other | | | | | | | |
| 1.3 Total resources for patient services | | | | | | | |
| 2. Planned Expenditure | | | | | | | |
| 2.1 Category A – Block Contracts | | | | | | | |
| 2.2 Category B – Cost-per-Case/Cost and Volume | | | | | | | |
| 2.3 Total patient services expenditure | | | | | | | |
| 3. Income and Expenditure Patient Services | | | | | | | |
| SECTION B | | | | | | | |
| 4.1 Drugs Monies – Resources Available | | | | | | | |
| 4.2 Drugs Monies – Expenditure | | | | | | | |
| 5.1 Practice Staff – Resources Available | | | | | | | |
| 5.2 Practice Staff – Expenditure | | | | | | | |
| 6.1 Other use of savings – Resources Available | | | | | | | |
| 6.2 Other use of savings – Expenditure | | | | | | | |

COMPLETED BY:                    TEL No:

Figure 8.2 cont.

# 9  All Roads Lead to ROME: The Regional Role in Fundholding

## Geoff Meads

## Regional role

On 13 January 1994 the Minister of Health, Dr Brian Mawhinney, took the unusual step of writing personally to all fundholders. Following the Government's announcement that District and Family Health Services Authorities (FHSAs) were to be merged from 1 April 1996 he sought to allay widespread concern amongst general practice that these new 'Health Commissions' were not about to assume a direct line management responsibility for fundholding. The concern arose because the Government announcement also made clear that 1 April 1996 was also the target date for implementing legislation to abolish RHAs: the statutory guardians of fundholding since its inception. Dr Mawhinney's reassurances to fundholders were simple and straightforward: for RHA read ROME (Regional Office of the NHS Management Executive), with all the previous Regional responsibilities to promote and protect the development of fundholding as the competitive edge in local purchasing, only more so. In short, the regional role remains *in loco parentis*.

## Regional approach

In his letter Dr Mawhinney described fundholding as still in its infancy, offering the tantalizing prospect of an adolescence when a range of increasingly vigorous primary care-led purchasing initiatives grow into an adulthood where the most robust of these largely replace the functions of DHAs themselves. Such a maturation requires good parenting by Regional Offices of the infant fundholder: wise counsel, encouragement, guidance and, as ever, a sensible balance between care and control. Like books on parentcraft, fundholding regulations are sound mostly in theory and best left largely on the shelf for use only in cases of last resort.

The effective operation of the fundholding scheme depends on Regional Offices, even as part of the central Executive, reading between the lines and ensuring that as with the individual general medical services (GMS) contract, the most detailed regulatory framework in the NHS does not get translated into burdensome bureaucracy. The regional 'light touch' required for Hospital and Community Health Services Trusts applies equally well to general practice fundholders: they should be seen to occupy comparable positions as NHS 'providers'. It is essential that, across regions, fundholders have the scope to develop and diversify in ways that will lead ultimately to the extended primary care team replacing the hospital as the focal unit for the NHS investment in health and health care.

## Regional responsibilities: specific

There are nevertheless some 'bottom lines'. These are the unequivocal requirements of regional management. Within the reformed NHS it is the direct responsibility of ROME to:

- approve general practice applications for fundholding status
- set fundholding annual budgets
- oversee overall fundholding performance, including the scrutiny of individual fundholder decisions where required
- handle fundholder over- and under-spends
- respond to fundholder appeals and
- support fundholder withdrawals from the scheme where appropriate.

These six functions are not for delegation[1]. Whilst each one of them requires close and effective collaboration with local health authorities it is essential both for the individual fundholder and for the NHS as a whole that these responsibilities remain at the regional level.

For the individual fundholder the regional level of responsibility is the guarantee of fair play. ROME's task is to assure equitable allocations between fundholders and other purchasers, between primary and acute care providers, and across the whole range of prescribers. It is to construct a regulatory framework from a platform of policies which continuously draw on the fundholding experience in proportion to its growth. Above all ROME is there to protect the integrity and independence of the fundholding practice itself. It is axiomatic to the NHS reforms that the individual GP, acting for his or her patient whether as provider or purchaser, is free to take decisions in the best interests of that patient.

For the NHS as a whole regional management is equally important. ROME is charged by the Executive of the NHS with its performance management. Whilst the overall framework for the NHS, its culture, values and identity are centrally determined, the delivery of national objectives and priorities depends on the targets set and agreed regionally within purchasers' corporate contracts and providers' business plans. It is at ROME that there is the regional overview which ensures that all communities have access to the full range and level of NHS services. Independent contractor fundholders certainly are, and must remain so, but within the framework of the NHS. Unilateral declarations of independence are the job of ROME to prevent and if necessary to veto. Summary dismissals from the fundholding scheme remain a statutory regional power[2] – never yet exercised but an essential reminder that the potential for unplanned services and long-term fragmentation inherent in the separation of purchasing responsibilities requires constant vigilance at ROME.

Inevitably and rightly this means a dedicated fundholding team in the Regional Office. Fundholding management at any level requires different levels and types of professional contribution throughout the NHS annual cycle. At the start of the summer it is the policy-makers in the ascendancy as the various planning guidance drafts are issued. In the autumn information analysts take over to assess the outputs from the fundholding data capture period and supply material to the medical advisers and management accountants, who work through the winter months to recommend finally the fundholders' budgets by the end of January. And then comes the spring with budget offers and contract signing, and regional mediators waiting in the wings to conciliate and arbitrate if called upon. Fundholding is a classic example of NHS matrix working.

Effective co-ordination of these widely differing functions requires high-quality management. So too does the sum of monies involved: over £500 million in many regions. An overall 'fundholding programme manager' is accordingly a fixed point in the organizational structure of ROME, most closely linked to the primary care development and performance management departments but never, in reality, far from the Regional Chief Executive's office. Of all ROME's functions fundholding is both the most labour-intensive challenge and, particularly given its political origins, the most potentially fallible as a result. Prudent RHA members have required monthly briefings on potential fundholding flashpoints in their private meetings.

## Regional responsibilities: strategic

The extent to which fundholding requires operational responsibility to be held at regional level is highly unusual, and many of the problems the scheme encountered in its early years can be attributed to RHAs' lack of experience and expertise in managing a development that required such a specific 'hands-on' approach. ROME is by definition part of the NHS headquarters and as such part of its strategic management. Its home ground is ensuring that the overall pattern of financial and human resources is correct. For fundholders it is important to be aware of this strategic management context, not least because it can mean they are uniquely placed to influence and take advantage of associated developments in the wider NHS.

This applies most obviously in the area of funding policy. It is ROME's function to assess the overall revenue allocation required by the fundholders in its region; but only after having first been part of the Executive's decision-making process on the level of annual public expenditure settlement to be sought for the NHS and the formula to be applied for capitation-based allocations. These are of critical concern to fundholders.

For example, as the previously separate General Medical Service (to FHSAs) and hospital and community health services (to DHAs) allocations converge, and as capitation benchmarks increasingly become baselines for fundholders' budgets, it is important that they are locally sensitive. This requires a funding policy which gives due weight to, for example, patient morbidity and mobility and not just to age and deprivation factors. It also requires allocations by ROME that are both demonstrably even handed, through for example identical inflation uplifts to District Authorities; and consistent with ROME's strategic responsibility for primary care development. Negotiations between Health Authorities and fundholders on the latter's effective contribution to the NHS Efficiency Index, and specific increases in activity set as targets at District levels, are therefore perfectly legitimate requirements of ROME; but in the context of securing these increases from primary care settings as the shift from the institutional acute sector is further promoted. It is equally appropriate for ROME to provide fundholders and Health Authorities with different levels of financial increase. Individual fundholders' budgets, for example, already reflect capital charges because they are based on provider tariffs. For Districts increases in capital charges have to be financed directly from growth.

The significance of overall allocation policies to fundholding, as exercised by ROME, applies to capital as well as revenue arrangements. It is again the regional role to advise on the national requirements for capital and to approve individual schemes within a properly co-ordinated overall programme. NHS capital is not the sole property of NHS Trusts. The rules guiding its application to the independent sector for purposes of care in the community and primary care development have been significantly strengthened in recent years. Several RHAs by the end of 1993 had introduced specific categories in their capital programmes for primary care infrastructure developments. In regions such as Wessex these offered the prospect of up to 50 new surgery and health centre developments over the 1993–98 period on top of those already planned through cost rent and improvement grant mechanisms by FHSAs. The business plans of fundholding practices, as the pioneers for extended primary care teams, were a vital source for these proposed developments.

Finally, in this section, it is important to remember that the strategic management of ROME applies to human as well as financial resources, and in particular to professional development. The development of clinical audit, professional advice on future medical and management personnel requirements, and the purchasing of most postgraduate education and training, are functions of ROME. Fundholding is only one component of the organizational development of the NHS, but because of its position at the cutting edge of the health-care market place the scheme is of particular significance. It is to fundholding practices that ROME looks for evidence of future changes in skills mix: the increases in numbers of physiotherapists and the realignment of community nurses, for example, and the whole movement towards unified primary care teams and inter-professional education as a result. It is the new fund and practice consortia managers who are now most sought after by universities' rapidly expanding health service management schools.

Above all the direct relationship of fundholders to ROME offers them the unique opportunity to guide the future direction of the NHS. The national strategic development fund, for ministerial and other central initiatives, is still to be regionally allocated and administered. Fundholding practices are in effect national demonstration sites. For government they can see a thousand flowers bloom.

## Operational context

The very numbers involved in fundholding and their steady annual expansion since 1990 compel local delegation by ROME. Decisions about levels of computer reimbursement, the practice-level application of different capitation benchmarks and the local requirements for practice staffing simply cannot be taken sensibly on a regional basis. Essential operationally for the smooth running of the fundholding scheme, local delegation is equally important for the operational dividend it brings in terms of collaboration and cohesion within the wider reformed NHS.

For, in reality, whilst arms-length agencies can be considered ROME has little option but to delegate fundholding management tasks to local Health Authorities, particularly as, in many regions, the management of Districts and FHSAs are increasingly brought together in 'Health Commissions' (HCs). These represent the regional opportunity to ensure that, however competitive local contracting may be, it is all driven by shared health and health-care priorities in line with overall NHS objectives. For, as Table 9.1 illustrates[4], the potential for outright conflict between fundholders and other purchasers is deeply rooted not simply within the terms of reference of the scheme, but in their very different cultures and origins.

This potential for conflict requires ROME to ensure a rigorous annual business cycle for the local management of delegated functions. Collaboration on purchasing plans and ensuring the best overall value for money in the allocation of resources has to be made mandatory: as inherent in the system as competition is to the contracting period with providers in the first 3 months of each calendar year. The key to collaboration in the preceding 9 months is the specific regional requirement for such agreed outcomes between Health Authorities and fundholders as those listed below, in a timetable based on the approach adopted in the South and West Region.

- *April* – Combined plans for surgery/health centre developments, following practice acceptance of fund offers.
- *May* – Health Authority confirmation of final fundholding budgets and signed contracts with providers.
- *June* – Out-turn reviews endorsing use of planned savings for shared priorities in primary care.
- *July* – Download of District and FHSA data to practices for completion of, for example, practice staff and referral profiles for GP annual reports.

**Table 9.1** NHS purchasers: compare and contrast

| Health Authorities | | Fundholders |
|---|---|---|
| 1 Population based and community oriented. | *versus* | Oriented to individuals, families and special needs. |
| 2 Focus on overall health needs. | *versus* | Driven by patient demand. |
| 3 Salaried staff usually on permanent contracts. | *versus* | Self-employed reliance on annual business dividend. |
| 4 Secure sources of recurrent NHS capital and revenue. | *versus* | Variable income levels from range of contracts including insurance companies, occupational health schemes and bank overdrafts. |
| 5 Funding via weighted capitation formulae. | *versus* | Motivated financially by achieving higher volumes of fees, allowances and screening targets, with GPFH allocations based on historic patterns of Hospital and Community Health Services (HCHS) usage. |
| 6 Employee status staff and management with frequently changing functions who can lack real sense of ownership of Health Authorities (or HCs). | *versus* | Power and money belongs to the practices where professional roles and responsibilities are relatively constant. |
| 7 Long history of working with local authorities, often unproductively and sometimes collusively. | *versus* | Often an anathema historically to local authorities, whose councillors can be threatened by loss of control inherent in GPFH/care management alliances and devolved budgets. |
| 8 Belong to modern EU political culture of (sub) regional strategic planners. | *versus* | Characteristic of UK modern political culture of the new consumerism. |

**Table 9.1** *continued*

| Health Authorities | | Fundholders |
|---|---|---|
| 9 Appointed statutory membership represents traditional public authority and accountability. | *versus* | Popular support and patient 'stakeholders' offer real 'democratic' alternative to legitimize public services. |
| 10 Can be perceived as remote from the public they claim to champion. | *versus* | In daily direct contact with users and carers, 24-hour access. |
| 11 Have required regular and detailed performance management rather than regulation. | *versus* | Entrepreneurial businesses, privately owned, fit for the (health care) market place. |
| 12 Report to intermediate tier via formal chains of command and management channels. | *versus* | Direct access to Department of Health and Ministers for GPFH/GMSC leadership. |
| 13 Identified with long waiting lists, hospital crises and low efficiency. | *versus* | Unprecedented levels of planned savings, prescribing under-spends and 100% target achievement. |
| 14 Purchasing has so far served risk management and cost containment rather than real health gain or general shifts from acute care. | *versus* | Really promote primary care and serve as a vehicle for central policy in aligning providers with health objectives. |
| 15 Regarded by many as a transitional organizational phase *en route* to universal primary care-led purchasing. | *versus* | Here to stay: yesterday, today and tomorrow. |

- *August* – Public health support to fundholders in preparing health plans.

- *September* – Issue of health authority purchasing intentions based on practice health plans.

- *October* – Joint mid-year reviews apply in-year under-spends to shared priorities.

- *November* – Practice-level negotiations on activity and quality targets for joint use in contracting round.

- *December* – Practice approval for use of specific capitation benchmarks in fundholder draft activity offers.

The above list is by no means exhaustive but its timetable format does clearly highlight the careful and conscientious approach to collaboration required. With DHAs reliant on fundholders as their primary source of intelligence for their new responsibilities, but with these responsibilities still covering the most serious secondary care referrals made by general practice, their need for each other is actually far greater today than it was before the NHS reforms were introduced in 1991.

## Policy context

Before their merger on 1 April 1994 most of the then 14 RHAs had published strategies or strategic frameworks for primary care development. Whilst, in some cases, these documents represented a first-time discovery of the family health services by Regions the common policy thrust that could be discerned was towards extended primary care teams established through augmenting the nationally negotiated contract for individual GPs with local service level agreements. This move towards practice-based contracts has also been identified by the General Medical Services Committee nationally[5], and its initial opposition to the concept has itself attracted considerable criticism from GPs who, by April 1994, had already responded to Regional policies by agreeing wider roles and responsibilities for their practices with local Health Authorities and HCs. It was clear that, whatever the outcome of the debate, the principle of primary care-led purchasing in the NHS had become established.

Primary care-led purchasing is a direct consequence of the fundholding scheme. It is not, of course, always the same, and sometimes local initiatives on primary care-led purchasing are deliberately designed by practices or Health Authorities as alternatives to fundholding. Conversely, fundholders themselves can become involved in local purchasing developments that substantially extend beyond the strict wording of the scheme's regulations. A Regional typology of primary care-led purchasing which describes its different stages is as follows:

1 Input from individual practices to Health Authority or HC purchasing decisions.

2 Input from groups of general practices representative of a Health Authority or HC area to purchasing decisions.

3 Combinations of local primary health care teams (PHCTs) come together to influence purchasing decisions.

4 Local PHCTs compile individual health plans for submission to a Health Authority or HC to influence purchasing decisions.

5 Combinations of local PHCTs compile one health plan to influence purchasing decisions.

6 Individual PHCTs compile a health plan as a basis for being allocated indicative budgets by a Health Authority or HC, but with purchasing still directly undertaken by the latter.

7 Combinations of local PHCTs compile a health plan to influence purchasing decisions and bid for contracts for shared services at practice levels.

8 Individual PHCTs or groups of PHCTs compile a local health plan and receive allocations for the purchase and provision of agreed services.

9 Combinations of local PHCTs compile a local health plan and social care plan and receive allocations from a Health Authority or HC for the purchase and provision of agreed services. Staff may be employed within the PHCTs as care managers with a limited budget for social care.

10 Combinations of local PHCTs compile a local health and social care plan and receive allocations delegated by a Health Authority or HC and Social Services Department for the purchase and provision of agreed services.

The ten stages often overlap in their actual implementation and practices may develop across several stages at any one time. Nevertheless the typology may be understood, by both practioners and purchasers, as a broadly chronological sequence[6].

All fundholders should be at least at stage 8 to operate effectively within the national policy and regulatory requirements for the scheme, completing tasks inherent in the earlier stages automatically as integral parts of a fundholder's annual business cycle. In reality, many fundholders press ROME to be at stages 9 and 10 and with Dr Mawhinney's successor as Minister of Health, Dr Gerry Malone, proposing total and community purchasing options for GPs by 1996, progressive extensions to the fundholding scheme can therefore confidently be anticipated.

The regional policy perspective is that secondary and, to a lesser extent, social care will increasingly be purchased from primary care agencies funded, through locally weighted capitation formulae, for this purpose. This policy is likely to leave Health Authorities with a residual direct purchasing role, and a chief local responsibility for the negotiation and management of local contracts with general practice and other primary care providers.

In other words, the roles and responsibilities of the pre-1991 NHS will have been completely turned on their heads by the introduction of the fundholding scheme and its associated reforms.

# References

1   *Progress Report – Managing the New NHS. Detailed Analysis of Functions.* NHS Management Executive. February 1994, pp. 33–43.
2   *National Health Service (Fund Holding Practices) Regulations 1993.* Statutory Instrument No 567, Part IV.
3   *Health Authority Payments in Respect of Social Services Functions.* HSG(92)43, Annex C, NHS Act 1977, Section 28A.
4   Competition or collaboration? *Primary Care Management* (1994), **4**(3): 2.
5   *Report for Discussion. Practice Based Contracts.* General Medical Services Committee. January 1994.
6   *A Strategic Framework for Primary Care.* Wessex Regional Health Authority Public Consultation Paper. December 1993.

# 10 The Provider Perspective

## *Paul Lambden*

## Introduction

For the providers of health care the reforms introduced fundamental changes which struck at the very heart of the way in which they had previously operated. All providers of medical services could become Trusts, unfettered by District and Regional bureaucracy, free to appoint their own staff, to develop as they felt appropriate, to acquire and dispose of their own assets and to manage themselves. However, 43 years of provider-driven care were also replaced with a purchaser-driven system which demanded responsiveness from the providers and from their medical staff. No longer would it be acceptable for hospital consultants to dictate the way in which they would provide their services but the purchasing authorities would agree, through contracts, what services they would require. In other words the assignment of priorities in health care and the rationing of finite resources would be the responsibility of the purchaser. The size of this burden still has not been fully understood by some purchasers. However, for optimal use of funding, the clinician with responsibility for the overall care of the patient must also have the financial responsibility and, for that reason, the fundholding initiative has been very successful. The GP fundholders have purchased much more effectively than the DHAs and, because of much greater understanding of the needs of individual patients, have used their entrepreneurialism to achieve innovative improvements in service which have reduced waiting times, improved access, raised quality and reduced costs.

## Consultant attitudes

Although it was understood that consultants were not God, for some the distinction was so fine that it was felt not to matter. The reforms brought sharply into focus the fact that they were employees required to respond to purchaser requirements. Many consultants have accepted the reforms enthusiastically. They have examined the services which they provide and, in consultation with the GPs, have produced much more appropriate and patient-sensitive care, for example by offering outreach services. In general the patients have received better care and the provider has been successful if its consultants have adopted an enlightened view.

Sadly, this has not been the case everywhere. Some consultants have opposed the reforms in every way possible, still rooted in the stultifying traditions of pre-reform medical provision, refusing to adhere to contract requirements, refusing to meet targets for admission, refusing to acknowledge the more comprehensive GP appreciation of patient requirements. They have regarded purchasers in general and fundholders in particular as an evil in the provision of health care, and the most extreme have vowed to fight to the death the dominance of the purchaser. Those consultants risk bringing about their own demise and potentially the loss of their own hospitals. It is quite clear that, with modern developments in medicine, there will be reductions in hospitals all round Britain, and those remaining will be used much more efficiently. The consultants who have recognized the benefits of the reforms will dynamically and flexibly meet the challenges whilst the anti-reform consultants, like King Canute, will be 'drowned' by the tide of change.

Many consultants who still regard the reforms with reluctance cite the two-tier service as their main objection. They regard as iniquitous the fact that patients of non-fundholders appear to be waiting longer in many instances than the patients of fundholders and they fail to recognize that, far from the service worsening for non-fundholders, it has actually improved considerably for the fundholders because of their ability to be innovative and to negotiate sharp and effective contracts with providers. They have yet to understand that, with multiple purchasers, there will be different priorities assigned to different types of cases and therefore different waiting times will be an integral part of care provision depending on a range of clinical and financial factors of which only the purchasers may be aware.

# Dealing with Clinical Directors and business managers

The Clinical Director, responsible for the clinical and financial management of his directorate, first appeared in about 1987 and the model of clinical management has now been adopted by the vast majority of hospital and community consultant units nationwide. It has been a difficult time within specialties as the consultants have realized that they are no longer independent practitioners within the secondary care system but have responsibilities to meet clinical and financial targets and to work to agreed protocols and guidelines. Failure to meet those requirements now results in sanctions which may range from the loss of beds or operating sessions to redundancy. It has, however, provided an unparalleled opportunity to improve efficiency and value-for-money within the clinical specialties as medical practices have been modified to take into account cost as well as best practice. Indeed there have been many examples where quality of provision has either been unaffected or even enhanced whilst reducing costs.

In most hospitals the decisions about day-to-day operation are now in the hands of the Clinical Directors together with the Chief Executive, and this has resulted in much more effective units operating within a more appropriate clinical framework.

The Clinical Director also works with the business manager to manage the provision of services both within the unit and to the GP customers. They will work together in deciding what services are to be offered, calculating the costs of those services, establishing the prices to be charged to the purchasers, negotiating the contracts and resolving any difficulties which might arise with service delivery. The business manager also markets the available services to the GPs. This is a central function because the ultimate viability of any unit depends on fully funded utilization of the available resources. Indeed as hospital facilities are used more efficiently (i.e. more intensively and for longer hours) and medical advances (for example laparoscopic surgery) reduce bed stays, the number of beds (and therefore the number of hospitals) required will diminish. In simple terms, viability will depend directly on the number of pairs of feet walking through the doors. Meeting the requirements of GPs on behalf of their patients is the only sure way to guarantee the survival of any unit.

## The contracts manager

Contracting has become the single most important managerial activity within any Trust or Directly Managed Unit. The contract governs the amount of work to be undertaken, the price to be paid for that work and the conditions and constraints to be applied to both the provider and the purchaser. Negotiation is usually long and hard and, since the introduction of the reforms, has been the source of many of the difficulties with the new system, largely because of inexperience (and occasionally incompetence) within the negotiating teams. It is also quite clear that purchasing skills, particularly in DHAs, have lagged behind provider skills, resulting in major inequalities in negotiating ability which have favoured the providers. The contracts manager is an integral part of the negotiating team and he will draft the contracts (more properly termed service agreements), lead discussions about areas of contention, monitor the activity of the contract from the provider perspective and keep abreast of information published by the management executive about changes in contracting generally.

## Six-month rules and cycle/planning changes in contracts

At present contracts for services agreed between the providers of health care and the purchasers (both Health Authorities and GP fundholders) are renewed annually. This is a most unsatisfactory situation because the period of operation is too short to make effective changes in service provision, funding for few developments being able to be recouped within a year. To develop patterns of care and to demonstrate their effectiveness a minimum of 2 or 3 years is required and contract terms need to run for this time. Contracts negotiated on an annual basis are not a feature of any other area of business or industry. However, this 'short-termism' is generated from the centre because allocations to purchasers are made annually and no purchaser is prepared to commit funding to particular projects until the extent of money available is known. The only compromise which could reconcile these difficulties would be to agree (say) annual contracts with a 3-year commitment, but without the actual funding for years two and three being known. This would, at least, ensure a period of stability within any unit.

At present contract changes can be made with 6 months' notice. This does give some time to the provider to make arrangements to increase or reduce staff and to adjust facilities according to demand, although the notice period itself is short when major redirection in referrals is planned.

As purchasers embark on competitive tendering exercises for major elements of service, adjustment of estates and staff will be undertaken more frequently. However, if such a policy is operated the purchasers must remember that two possible consequences may arise to cause major difficulties subsequently.

- For any NHS provider a large element of prices is the fixed capital element and, in the event of a service being transferred to another hospital, it may not be possible for the provider to rapidly divest those costs. This will result in higher prices for the remaining services as the full costs are spread over a smaller range of specialties. Indeed some providers, particularly specialist providers, have actively adopted a differential price loading policy and charge very high prices for specialist procedures, for which there are only a limited number of suppliers, and much lower prices for routine procedures. Purchasers will have to be very careful that centralizing services on limited sites does not result in higher prices for other services.

- It may not be possible to reprovide a service after it has been transferred elsewhere when the premises have been used for an alternative purpose and the equipment and the staff have been dispersed. The consequence will be that fewer sites only will be able to offer particular facilities and a near monopoly situation will be created removing purchaser manoeuvrability and inevitably resulting in increased prices consequent on 'rarity value' of the service.

## Monitoring performance

Until the introduction of the reforms the supplier of health services was also the holder of the funds for the provision of those services. A cosy cartel therefore existed which protected the Health Authority from any criticisms by patients because it had the responsibility for the totality of service delivery. Under the reformed Health Service arrangements the provider of health care receives funds from the purchasing fundholders and Health Authorities, who also have a responsibility to monitor the quality of the services provided together with the way in which the provider delivers the contracts which have been agreed. Monitoring performance is by examination of standards which are agreed within the contract negotiations.

- Have the agreed numbers of emergency and urgent patients been seen and treated?

- Has the elective contract been fulfilled?
- Have Patient's Charter and other standards been met?
- Has the provider supplied the agreed reports about activity?

In successive years the purchaser will be expecting increasing quality standards combined with shorter waiting times. The standards of NHS care should therefore rise inexorably but it is important that all purchasers should remember the quality triangle and understand the principle that cost, quality and quantity of care are inextricably bound. It is not feasible to increase quality of care or the number of patients treated without the injection of money (except in those circumstances where medical advances of themselves reduce costs, e.g. minimally invasive surgery). Similarly, reducing the money available will result in declining numbers of patients treated or a deterioration in quality.

There is also the problem of what constitutes quality. Patients like courtesy and reasonable time-keeping. They like to wait to be seen in a waiting room and not in a draughty corridor, they like health service buildings to be clean and they like a reasonable standard of food if they are admitted. The patients' perceptions are very important if a unit is to be successful. Equally important, however, is the purchaser's more clinically orientated requirements. They include the delay in out-patient consultation and in-patient admission, the arrangement for specimen collection and the speed of return of test results, the percentage of consultations undertaken by the consultant, the quality and availability of communications, in-patient standards, readmission rates and mortality and morbidity statistics, the quality of the discharge letter and the speed with which it is supplied. Therein lies the greatest of all problems. There are myriad measures of quality and to subject to scrutiny more than a fraction would be inefficient, ineffective and horrendously time consuming. The result would be a discredited and valueless exercise.

For success, therefore, quality needs to be assessed by a few relevant and clear-cut parameters which can be measured and quantified, supported, if appropriate, by patient satisfaction surveys.

## The waiting list

A fundamental change occurred with the inception of the reforms: the loss of the consultant's responsibility for the waiting list. Prior to 1991, patients would be referred by the GP and would be seen and investigated by the consultant. If an admission was deemed to be appropriate, the patient would be added to a list maintained by the consultant and endorsed with a suitable degree of urgency. When the patient's turn arrived he would be called for admission. Everything has changed now. Most purchaser contracts specify that all emergency and urgent patients should be treated and urgency is defined by one or more criteria laid down by the purchaser. Those awaiting a routine admission, however, can be invited for treatment only if the purchaser agrees.

The population still does not appreciate generally that the constraints within the system are now applied by the purchasers. However much spare capacity a hospital may have, however keen the hospital may be to undertake a particular treatment, or however much a consultant may wish to admit a particular person, only the purchaser can authorize that admission through a contract agreement.

As purchasing becomes more refined there will increasingly be 'initiatives' which will result in individual groups being selected for surgery out of chronological order. For example, a purchaser may choose to eliminate (say) the list of patients waiting for a hip replacement with a specific tranche of money. Other patients, for other orthopaedic procedures, may have to wait much longer. None of this will be exclusively within the hospital's control and that must be fully understood. Consultants experience great difficulty in managing the patients who lobby them for admission when the responsibility lies partly outside their control. Initiative purchasing will undoubtedly encourage better treatment, more effectively and with greater value for money, but the consequences must be fully appreciated in order to minimize disquiet.

## Special provider initiatives and non-contract (one-off) work

The provider staff, through their contacts with the various purchasers, are often able to gauge better than anyone else the requirements of the population which they serve. This is particularly true with respect to the DHA, which cannot possibly enjoy the same well-informed relationship with the population as the provider who provides the care. As a result of this close association gaps in the market, areas where additional services are required and which could profitably be added, are recognized and the provider may, as an initiative, develop such services for marketing to the Districts and to the fundholders. There are difficulties with such developments; raising any required capital is difficult if the return is not within the same financial year; purchaser support is required and it is unclear whether this should be obtained in advance of developing new services (with the attendant risk of competitor provider units discovering plans and acting to defeat the initiative) or after the service is completed (with the risk that they might not give support and purchase elsewhere). However, with further development of the fundholding initiative there will undoubtedly be increasing numbers of schemes designed to meet the requirements of the fundholders.

Initiatives may also take the form of blocks of treatment provided, usually to fundholding practices, and often discounted by undertaking the work at marginal costs. A block of, for example, 50 elective surgical procedures at (say) half price to fill a space in theatre and ward time, notably towards the end of the financial year, is becoming commonplace and is a valid and efficient use of spare capacity. This additional work may also be undertaken in response to tendering enquiries by any of the purchasers although poor tendering reveals a serious defect in such a policy. If a purchaser invites tenders for a block of work and, if a provider quotes for that work at a price which is below cost, then clearly the provider will slip into deficit through undertaking it. This will jeopardize the viability of the provider and may ultimately result in the loss of the service or, if the provider is rescued by transitional relief from the centre, will damage other providers which quote on the basis of a sound financial base. Furthermore transitional relief is a very poor means of funding a provider because it is non-specific and there is no way of measuring whether the money invested gives good value. In no other area of commerce or industry would a firm quote for work at a price below cost. This must be monitored carefully by all purchasers to ensure that a short-term gain does not result in a longer-term loss of service or increased prices.

## Tertiary referrals

The issue of tertiary referrals is complex. GPs refer patients to the consultant of their choice but a proportion of the cases will be found to require a further referral to a particular specialist centre. Examples are to be found in those patients referred to a District General Hospital and sent on to cardiac or neurological centres. Tertiary referrals of this type may have significant financial implications. The fundholder may suddenly receive a large invoice for work which falls within the range of services covered by the fundholding initiative, albeit capped at a maximum of £6000. The District purchaser may find that, whatever contracts it sets, it has little control over tertiary referrals because NHS Executive guidance specifically permits extra-contractual tertiary referrals without restriction (HSG(93)8). It is very important that the issues surrounding tertiary referrals are rapidly resolved. Consultants feel that attempts to constrain their ability to make tertiary referrals are an unwarranted intrusion into their freedom to treat in the best way possible any patient sent to them. Yet the money which such referrals cost may seriously affect the money available for other treatments and, in consequence, a serious conflict of interests has emerged between the secondary care and the primary care practitioners. There is also a medico-legal dimension; if a consultant is constrained from making a tertiary referral and the patient suffers an adverse outcome, then the budget holder might be held to account – not a situation relished by any purchaser.

A resolution of this issue is essential. Perhaps the best arrangement is for consultants providing secondary care to agree with the purchasers, including the fundholders, a list of specialist units and consultants to which they would refer if a further opinion were required, together with a system of notification to the GPs which ensures that no unexpected invoices are received. There will still be some consultants wishing to use particular specialists or units which are excluded from the lists but no system linking clinical and financial issues can ever be entirely acceptable to everyone.

## A note of caution

The fundholding initiative is working extremely well and the fund-holders have, for the most part, been most effective purchasers achieving improvements through innovative and patient-focused contracts. Indeed in my experience they have been considerably better than the District purchasers with whom the Trusts also deal. However, there have been one or two practices which have been unreasonably pernickety and officious, refusing to pay any invoice with a spelling mistake, an in-correct date of birth or any other minor error. Although all providers strive for accuracy, attitudes of that sort will do nothing except force the system to grind to a halt. Furthermore not all errors are the fault of the provider; some are the result of incorrect information offered by the patient or the referring GP. If the scheme is not to suffer any sort of discreditation, it is important that co-operation occurs and realism triumphs at the expense of paranoia.

## Conclusion

The reforms have changed the way in which health care is provided within the NHS. They have improved quality of care, stimulated the development of new facilities and have awoken the entrepreneurial giant of the fundholder. They have released the hospitals from their previous bureaucracy by the introduction of Trust status and, subject to the centre not regaining control and stifling developments, will ensure that secondary care flourishes with better standards and value for money.

President John F. Kennedy said, in 1963, 'He who looks only to the past or the present is sure to miss the future'. His prophetic statement could not be more true than within the Health Service, where the future surely holds great opportunities to make the best health care in the world even better.

# 11  Financial Activity Reports

## *Bob Senior*

Many people find the multitude of reports provided by fundholding systems daunting. The distinction between Fund Statements, Fund Schedules and Fund Reports seems at first glance unclear. In essence the Fund Statements are intended to be the primary Financial Reports with the Fund Schedules providing details of how some of the figures contained in the Fund Statements are made up. The Fund Reports are then intended to provide activity information and supplementary financial information. The current list is as follows:

- Fund Statements:
  - Income and Expenditure Account (FIEA)
  - Savings Account (FSA)
  - Balance Sheet (FBS)
  - Income & Expenditure and FHSA Payments Forecast (FIEFPF)
  - Cash Payments Analysis (FCPA).

- Fund Schedules:
  - Hospital Services Expenditure Summary
  - Analysis of Proportion of Staff Costs
  - Analysis of Public Sector Debtors and Creditors
  - Analysis of Private Sector Debtors and Creditors
  - Analysis of Other Current Assets
  - FHSA (Responsible) Account
  - General Practice Current Account
  - Analysis of Other Current Liabilities
  - HCHS Payment Remittance Advice
  - Nominal Ledger Audit Trail
  - Nominal Ledger Batch Print
  - Analysis of Community Nursing Costs
  - Trial Balance.

- Fund Reports:
  - Block Referrals Analysis
  - Referral Exception Report
  - Hospital Services Accruals
  - Claim for Treatment Costs Over £6000
  - Patient Referral Costs Audit Trail
  - Analysis of Referral Costs by Treatment Type
  - Analysis of Treatments – By Hospital
  - Analysis of Treatments – Summary
  - Current Year Commitments
  - Future Year Commitments
  - Treatment Referral Costs Audit Trail.

You should remember that not all of these reports are intended to be used by the practice, and indeed some of those that are do not need regular attention.

## Reports used by others

Some reports related to the timing of payments are mainly intended for use by the FHSA/Health Commission.

- *Fund Statement 4* – Income & Expenditure and FHSA Payments Forecast
- *Fund Statement 5* – Cash Payments Analysis
- *Fund Statement 6* – FHSA (Responsible) Account

As the practice has no control over when cheques are actually issued it has little use for the first two of these. The information is, however, needed further up the NHS line of command when cash limits do start to apply. To all practical intents and purposes practices simply need to print those reports each month and send them off to the Family Health Services Authority (FHSA) or Health Commission (HC) for them to worry about. The third report is very much an audit trail for the FHSA/HC. As they actually issue cheques on the practice's behalf they maintain a set of books which shows how much they have paid out for each practice. Fund Statement 6 lists all the entries the practice believes have been processed, and can therefore be checked by the FHSA/HC against their actual records.

# Used for audit or checking purposes

Some of the reports are provided so that you can get specific items of information out of the software. You might want to do this to investigate a figure that looks wrong, to trace a transaction, or to answer a query, perhaps from the auditors. The reports that fall into this category are:

- *Fund Schedule 7* – General Practice Current Account
- *Fund Schedule 10* – Nominal Ledger Audit Trail
- *Fund Schedule 11* – Nominal Ledger Batch Print
- *Fund Schedule 13* – Trial Balance
- *Fund Report 1* – Block Referrals Analysis
- *Fund Report 5* – Patient Referral Costs Audit Trail
- *Fund Report 11* – Treatment Referral Costs Audit Trail.

# Reports used for management of the fund

When you have discounted the reports that are used by others, or used for audit or checking, the remaining reports are not too daunting. The degree of importance you should attach to these varies according to the time of year, some being more important at one time than another.

# Monthly reports

The order in which you work through the reports is not critical; however, following a logical course should guarantee that you do not overlook anything. A sensible order would be as follows.

### Fund Report 2 – Referral Exception Report

This is probably the most important report for you to work on regularly. It lists those referrals that, according to the expected treatment date, should have been commenced by now but have not. Regularly checking this report will help you find:

- whether the expected time to treatment on your contracts is reasonable

- those patients where the treatment was completed but was not chargeable
- patients who have moved or died
- patients who no longer want the operation
- most importantly, patients who have been treated but the provider has not told you anything about it.

You could ignore this report and do nothing about it. But if you do you will get a very nasty surprise when you get to the year end, as you cannot close the year with *any* items outstanding on this report! Much better therefore to work on the report each month than have to sort out perhaps 50–100 pages at the year end.

However, it is not worth wasting energy and time on this report for the period April to June–July because most fundholders are behind with their work at that time of year, either because the year end has delayed them or they have just started fundholding and there are a lot of data to process. There is no point working on this report until you are pretty much up to date, probably by the end of August.

## Fund Schedule 1 – Hospital Services Expenditure Summary

This is the first financial report you should look at. It shows the costs incurred for the month on the left-hand side of the page and the year to date on the right. It breaks the costs down between specialties but does not allow you to break the budget down, simply showing a total budget figure for all hospital services expenditure at the bottom of the report.

While the year-to-date figures are the ones you should focus on for judging the progress of the fund, since slight monthly variations get evened out as the year progresses, you should look at the current month figures to see if anything odd has happened. Typically, you would check that the costs for each specialty are reasonable for one month, looking for any where:

- there are zeros
- there are negative figures
- there are abnormally small or large figures.

A common mistake is to run the financial reports before provisionally closing the month. If this is done then there could easily be either zeros or negative figures for the month; check the date and time details at the end of the report to ensure that it shows either provisional or final closure.

If the month has been closed but there are zeros and you know referrals have been commenced, then check that the costs entered on any block or cost and volume contracts are correctly entered and not left as zero.

## Fund Statement 1 – Income and Expenditure Account (FIEA)

Again, this report shows the month's figures on the left-hand side of the page and the year to date on the right. It summarizes the financial performance of the fund showing the costs, and budgets, for each of the four main budget headings:

- Purchase of Hospital Services
- Drugs and Appliances Prescribed and Dispensed
- Proportion of Staff Costs
- Community Nursing.

There are two sets of figures on the right-hand side of the page for each heading. The upper row are the year-to-date values, as you would expect. The lower set, however, are a projection of the likely state of affairs for the whole year. This set of figures is calculated by taking the actual costs and budget for the year so far and adding to them the values entered for the remaining months of the year in the 'forecasting' routine. If therefore you go into the forecasting routine and project that you will underspend by 15% for the rest of the year, the lower set of figures will take that into account when looking at the likely financial result for the whole year. Therefore, only put serious estimates into the forecasting routines, *not* wild hopes! The figures for purchase of hospital services are brought forward from the total at the bottom of Fund Schedule 1, so you should check that the totals have been brought forward correctly.

There are four sections where what are effectively budget increases are brought in:

- Recovery of Patient Hospital Treatment Costs over £6000
- Further Fund Allocation (on material change)

- Transfer from FSA

- Supplementary Fund Allocation.

Any figures that appear should have arisen as a direct result of you making special postings, with paperwork being retained to back up the entries for the auditors to check.

The penultimate line on the report is 'Savings transferred to FSA'. This should only happen when you close the year: there should be no entries in here during the year.

### Fund Statement 2 – Savings Account (FSA)

This report shows the position on your savings, giving details of how they have been used during the year, any savings that have been returned, and how much remains unspent. You should check that any savings you use are reflected in this report, and remember that you actually have to make entries to reflect the use of savings.

### Fund Statement 3 – Balance Sheet (FBS)

This particular report often worries people more than the others; it need not. It simply attempts to show how the money that has been made available to the practice has been used and to agree the net money available to the current savings and FIEA under-spend.

The format of the report is daunting but you should remember that the format was designed to cater for a whole range of possible situations, many of which will not apply to you. Table 11.1 shows each line of the balance sheet with a brief note on its contents.

### Fund Schedule 8 – Analysis of Other Current Liabilities

Usually there are only two lines plus a total on this report. The first line is for 'Accruals – Deferred Budget', being that part of the budget that is allocated to the remaining months of the year. For example, if your budget was £2 400 000 for the year and you were looking at the reports for September, month 6, you would see October to March deferred with a figure of £1 200 000.

The second line, 'Accruals – Sundry Public Sector Creditors', can be more complex. The value shown is the balance on account 9904, the Public Sector Accruals account. It will normally be made up of the cost per case accruals as shown on Fund Report 3, plus any drugs estimate

**Table 11.1** Example of Fund Statement 3 – Balance Sheet (FBS)

| | £ | |
|---|---|---|
| *Assets* | | |
| Cash at bank | 0 | Should only have a value if you have an underspend on salaries |
| Debtors – Public Sector | 0 | Normally zero |
| – Private Sector | 0 | Normally zero |
| Other Current Assets | 0 | Normally zero |
| FHSA A/C (Responsible) | 100 000 | This is the amount of money held by the FHSA on your behalf. It is the value of any savings brought forward, plus the current year's budget, less *all* payments *made* on your behalf by the FHSA in the current year |
| General Practice Account | 0 | Normally zero – the practice is usually owed money and so the balance should be shown as a liability |
| | Assets 100 000 | |
| Less: | | |
| *Liabilities* | | |
| Creditors – Public Sector | 0 | This should reflect the value of invoices entered for NHS providers where the remittance advice has not been produced. If you run the remittance advices immediately before closing this should be zero |
| – Private Sector | 0 | As above, this should reflect the value of invoices entered for private providers where the remittance advice has not been produced |
| Other Current Liabilities | 90 000 | This is made up of the deferred budget (that proportion of the budget that relates to the remaining months of the year) and the amount of any accruals – see separate notes about Fund Schedule 8 |
| FHSA A/C (Responsible) | 0 | Normally zero – there would only be an amount in here if you have *over-spent* on the fund and the FHSA has paid out more than your budget |
| Cash at bank | 0 | Normally zero. You should not have an overdraft on the fundholding account |
| General Practice A/C | 0 | Normally zero, unless you have over-spent on Staff Costs in which case the over-spent amount will show here as an amount owing to the practice |
| | Liabilities 90 000 | |
| | Net assets/liabilities 10 000 | |

**Table 11.1** *continued*

| | | |
|---|---|---|
| Represented by: | | |
| Accumulated FSA Balance per Statement 2 | 5000 | Amount of unspent savings from earlier years. Zero in first year of fundholding |
| Accumulated FIEA Balance per statement 1 | 5000 | Current years under/(over) spend from the bottom of Fund Statement 1 |

NB: the total of these last two lines should equal the amount of Net Assets/Liabilities

that you might have entered. If you have made any other manual accruals they will be included in this figure as well. You should reconcile this figure with the total on Fund Report 3, plus any drugs estimate and manual accruals you might have made each month.

### Fund Report 6 – Analysis of Referral Costs by Treatment Type

This report breaks down your costs by specialty, by Office of Population Censuses and Surveys (OPCS) code with values for the current month and the year to date. While this information is useful the real importance of this report from a practical point of view is that it is one of the first the auditors will look at!

In normal circumstances the specialty totals on this report will agree with the figures on Fund Schedule 1, and the auditors will normally check that they agree. There are, however, circumstances where this might not happen; the most common is that an operator has uncommenced and cancelled a referral, as in some systems this results in the current month figures not agreeing. The less common situation is where a correction has been made by Direct Journal or manual accruals have been made. These things cause problems because of the different ways in which Fund Report 6 and Fund Schedule 1 are compiled (Figure 11.1).

There is no link between the Nominal Ledger and the files where the Fund Report 6 data are held. If you make any direct posting into the specialty accounts in the nominal ledger the values will not be reflected in Fund Report 6.

## Activity reports

Fund Reports 7, 7a, 8 and 8a provide you with valuable information about the activity of your providers and your waiting list. Both 'a' reports provide the same information as the main reports but analyse the

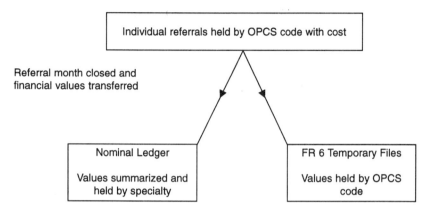

**Figure 11.1** Fund Report (FR) 6: relationship between individual referrals, Nominal Ledgers and Temporary Files

report between in-patient and day-case activity. All these reports can be produced for a specific period, for instance just for the last closed month, or for the months from April to the last closed month, say April to September. Generally producing the report for April to the last closed month gives the most useful information.

## Fund Report 7 – Analysis of Treatments – By Hospital

This report lists, by provider and then by specialty, all the procedures for which referrals have been made, or where a patient was waiting at the start of the period. The activity figures are provided under the following headings:

- Brought forward (on the waiting list at the start of the period specified)
- Commenced (procedure actually done in the period specified)
- Cancelled
- New (referrals made in the specified period)
- Carried forward (on the waiting list at the end of the specified period).

You can use this information to give you an overview of how your providers are performing and what is happening to your waiting list.

**Fund Report 8 – Analysis of Treatments – Summary**

This report gives exactly the same information as Report 7 but this time it is summarized across all providers. This version is useful for comparing overall activity with budgets and health plan targets, and monitoring your overall waiting-list position.

# The annual cycle

As the year progresses the reports that you need to concentrate on change, and they all increase in importance. The activity reports show whether your providers are likely to meet your activity targets, and whether your waiting lists need reducing. The financial reports will at the same time show how much money you are able to commit to extra activity. One report which starts to become relevant as you get to November and December is Fund Report 9 – Current Year Commitments.

This report lists, by month, those referrals that have expected treatment dates within the current year. It gives the patient's name and the expected cost of the treatment. It then gives the total accumulated for that patient for the current year and then any amount which exceeds the treatment cost limit for the year, i.e. £6000 for 1994–95. This report is obviously only any use if your expected treatment dates are reasonable. By the end of the calendar year the report will only be looking at the likely activity for the next 3 months. If you have been working on your Referral Exception Report regularly it should give a reasonable guide to the costs and activity for the rest of the year.

As you enter the last quarter of the year you will need to be monitoring very closely what is happening to any cost and volume or block with trigger contracts. The fundholding reports do not do too much to help you in this area, indeed they can be positively *misleading* if you have such contracts that are being over performed by the provider. The following section explains how this can happen, and how you can monitor the situation.

# 'Unallocated contracts'

Fund Schedule 1 – the Hospital Services Expenditure Summary – has a one-line entry at the foot of the report which is probably the biggest

'black hole' in the fundholding reports. This figure represents the under-
or over-used element of all your cost and volume or block (but not non-
attributable block) contracts. Each of these contracts has a control
account allocated to it when the contract is set up, with a number
between 5601 and 6000. As invoices for the block element of such
contracts are processed the amount paid is debited to the control
account. When referrals are commenced the cost of the referral is
credited to the control account and debited to the specialty to which it
relates, e.g. general surgery or out-patients.

If the control account has a debit balance on it (i.e. it is a positive
figure) this represents money you have paid out where the activity
performed has not used up the amount paid. In that situation there is
normally no amount repayable and hence the software writes the excess
paid off as an unspecified cost, adding it on to the true costs shown in
the rest of the report.

If, however, the contract is a cost and volume contract which is over-
performed, the negative figure that results (more has been taken out than
has been paid so far) really indicates that you will be receiving a further
invoice for the extra work before the end of the year. The software
regrettably does not distinguish between block and cost and volume contracts and assumes that all credit amounts are to be regarded as
deductions on Fund Schedule 1!

So what is the effect? A typical situation might be a cost and volume
contract with a community unit where you have not been told about all
activity and as a result £40 000 is still left as a debit, i.e. unused funds,
on that contract's control account. In the meantime your acute unit has
over-performed by £65 000 and that contract has a negative balance on
it. The software adds the two figures together and comes up with an
'Unallocated Contracts' total of minus £25 000. Your Fund Schedule 1
might then show costs before unallocated contracts of £525 000, which
after the credit is deducted become £500 000. If your budget so far is
£510 000 you are shown as having savings so far of £10 000. The true
position is that you should receive a further invoice from the acute unit
for £65 000. Were that to happen your true unallocated contracts figure
would have been a positive figure of £40 000, which when added to the
subtotal of £525 000 gives costs of £565 000 against a budget of
£510 000 – an *over-spend* of £55 000!

How do you check to see if you have this sort of problem? You
starting point is your Fund Schedule 13 – the Trial Balance. First divide
the balances between your providers and then identify any negative
balances on cost and volume or block with triggers contracts. If your
contracts do not allow for any such over-performance to be set off

against under-performance elsewhere then assume that a further invoice is due. Total up the amount of such further invoices due and then manually add that back to the total cost at the bottom of Fund Schedule 1. You will then have your true costs which you can compare with your budget.

## The audit

As a fundholder you will be visited by the auditors at the end of your first year, and then on an irregular basis in subsequent years. How regularly depends very much on how much, or little, trouble the auditors have with your records. What the auditors look at varies enormously; indeed they will deliberately look at different things each year. In general, however, their main concerns are over the following:

- Are the reports a true and fair picture of the fund's results for the year?

- Have the fundholding regulations been followed?

- Do figures in your accounts agree with figures elsewhere in the NHS, specifically:

  - is the budget correct?
  - does the FHSA responsible account agree with the FHSA's figures?
  - have amounts owed to providers been agreed with them?
  - have all costs been correctly accrued for?

- Are there any irregularities in the management allowance?

- What has happened to the level of staff salaries reimbursed?

To avoid problems with the auditors you need as a minimum to ensure that you follow the regulations set down by your FHSA/HC; sort out queries with providers and keep copies of any letters agreeing such queries; keep detailed records of your management allowance claims and copies of invoices; and generally keep your filing accurate and tidy. If you carry out the checks on your reports as explained above, and in particular that Fund Report 6 agrees with Fund Schedule 1, you should sort out any problems before the auditors pick them up.

## The year end

The year end is not something to be feared. While it is certainly a lot of hard work you can make life easier for yourself by working on some aspects as the year progresses.

- Work on Fund Report 2, the Referral Exception Report, each month and keep it down to as few entries as possible. It *must* be cleared before you can close the year.

- Go through Fund Report 3, the Hospital Services Accruals, each month and chase up providers for invoices.

- Agree activity levels with providers on a monthly basis.

- Ensure that the providers actually make any corrections for invoices that you have disputed as the year goes on.

- Reconcile the Accruals figure on Fund Schedule 8.

- Check Fund Schedule 6, the FHSA responsible account, each month to ensure that only invoices you have passed for payment, credit notes you have sent to the FHSA, or documented budget increases appear on it.

12 Fundholding and the Partners

*Stephen Henry and Lesley Morris*

It goes without saying that within a group practice there will be inevitable differences between human personalities. In fact the very strength of partnership in general practice relies on these differences. Recruiting and selecting a partner is often considered more difficult and of greater consequence than finding a suitable consort for marriage. Likewise if you seek an opinion from the nation's 30 000 GPs you will receive 30 000 different answers. At the same time each practitioner knows there are many different routes to effective treatment, or ways to reach an objective. Therefore within any partnership there will be stronger or weaker feelings towards the ethical and practical approaches to managing a slice of the nation's money and on behalf of the patient rather than the practice. Fundholding itself may still be considered a 'minority sport for the avant-garde' as in 1994 some 70% of GPs apparently think fundholding unethical and immoral and a denial of the true principles of a Bevanite Health Service.

## The lead partner

The lead partner will tend to be an avant-gardist, sufficiently motivated to strive for the better delivery of health care, someone who believes that he or she and the practice can take primary care on to a new plane by their direct management of the limited resources available. The prime quality must be enthusiasm closely coupled with optimism and the determination that, having set hands to the plough, whatever turns up in the way of imposed change of direction or financial complexity can be overcome. To this must be added the possibility that Health Authority officials may be lukewarm or even hostile to the scheme due to their perceived loss of authority. The lead partner must feel able, and be able, to convince not only all the members of the practice team but also all varieties of Health Authority staff and the patients with whom they deal, that the potential benefits are sound, the threats are without foundation, and that the practice can deliver its promises. He or she must also be capable of withstanding the brickbats of those opposed to the scheme face to face and in the medical and national press.

In many practices the lead has been taken by elder brethren who remember the lessons of 1948 and 1966 and who see clearly the opportunity to bring back the core of the Health Service to its grass roots origins. This is no way disbars the more energetic and altruistic younger members who may lack historical perspective but wish to drive what they may see as a more satisfactory vision of their future.

The lead partner needs to be aware of his or her partners' strengths and weaknesses and of the fact that GPs are usually chiefs and never indians. The role of *primus inter pares* is as subtle as a tight-rope walk across a minefield. As independent contractors the partners are effectively responsible only to themselves. Practice decisions are usually made only by compromise so corporate accountability may be very confused or vanish altogether unless well managed.

A study of ten practices in Newcastle suggested that the change to fundholding did not appear to affect established methods of decision-making. Decisions continue to be made by consensus. The practice manager acts as managing director in relation to a board of directors of the partners. The study highlighted difficulties of fostering a sense of corporateness. The problem was that key members of the workforce saw management control and discipline as secondary to their independent contractor status. On the one hand partners are directors of the board of management and on the other, part of the workforce. As such they are subject to the day-to-day management of their own decisions at the hands of their practice or fund manager. This relationship is now common within general practice but one with which the normal business culture is totally unfamiliar. It will become even more noticeable as the extended primary health care team (PHCT) of nursing and other disciplines seeks board-level representation.

Fundholding requires practices to visualize themselves as small businesses and to change 'people culture' into a more corporate approach. For investment purposes small businesses are currently defined as having an annual turnover of less than £0.5 million. Fundholding practices are well in excess of that figure and the word small may not be applicable. While most practices have used the practice manager and lead partner to develop the rapport needed between the professionals and the bureaucracy, this rather cosy situation may be less easy to maintain as the NHS internal market develops. As savings become harder to make and in an increasingly cash-limited environment, PHCTs will have to face up to the task of increasingly influencing the partners' decision making without curtailing their much-protected clinical and personal freedom.

The rise of the fund manager or the practice nurse to genuine partnership status is still some way off, but as fundholding itself becomes more of a business and the partners redefine their clinical status within the new corporate structure, the gradual acceptance of the management lead on clinical purchasing will take place (Figure 12.1).

## Monitoring systems and spreadsheets

In the beginning was Touche Ross and the first version of the fundholding software. This was commissioned as an accountancy tool for Health Service purposes so the specification was designed by accountants for accountants and to be Audit Commission friendly. Only as a secondary consideration was thought given to it being user useful as a management tool for the uninitiated. Accountants, like doctors,

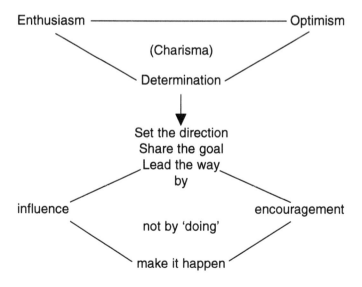

**Figure 12.1** Characteristics of the lead partner

somehow expect everyone to understand the basic principles on which their science is based. They remain, like doctors, genuinely surprised to find it is not so.

Most fundholding practices are accustomed to income and expenditure accounting, some even to balance sheets, but to this day double-entry book-keeping and chameleon-like accountancy debits and credits can paralyse the cerebral function of many fundholders (not so readily their fund managers), as quickly as hearing the question you prayed they would not ask in a viva-voce examination. No matter how often the meaning has been explained it is easily forgotten by the next morning.

The practice is required to understand and manage a running evaluation of its budget and the cost implications of the concept of accrual. For instance, in the purchasing of secondary care, at any moment there are patients in the pipeline between a referral and a consultation or waiting for a procedure as a result of a consultation or for follow-up appointments as a result of either. To each and every one of these episodes a price may be attached so there is a finite cost accruing to the practice as a result of the summation of these inevitabilities. Each annual or monthly cycle has accumulated a backlog of indebtedness against the current budget. At the same time the system is fluid and flexible. Referrals continue to be made, patients seen, operations performed and discharges completed. As there is only a small percentage leeway within the budget, unless one wishes to contemplate running into overdraft, the system must be shown to be on a positive or even balance.

In the preparatory year activity is essentially all that can be recorded as fundholders are without functioning fundholding software and even if they have it, its use in management is limited without a budget or tariffs.

It should be the partners' job to guide and advise the fundholding staff. If the fundholding staff are to provide the nuts and bolts of making things happen, all of the team need the answers to:

- Where are we now?
- Where do we want to go?
- How do we get there (what are the levers for change)?
- How do we know when we have arrived?

Answers to these questions service the business plan, thence the purchasing intentions, contracting and eventually outcomes. One of the functions of fundholding is to effect change. In collecting the activity of what is going on, where and in what numbers and to whom, a minimum list of data needs to be recorded.

- Patient's name
- Hospital number
- Date of birth
- GP
- Specialty
- Consultant
- Hospital
- Referral date
- First consultation (first seen date)

- Date on to waiting list
- Date operation done
- OPCS Code
- Cost
- Date(s) of follow-up(s)
- Date discharged
- Invoice details
- Date invoice paid

A spreadsheet is best used if this list of prospective as well as retrospective (proposed dates/actual occurrences) data are translated through all the specialty headings under secondary care, and then for direct access facilities (physiotherapy, etc.) and community headings (health visitor and district nurse contacts) as well as accident and emergency admissions and the internal workings of general medical services (minor surgery or midwifery, etc.). Most practices have found that approximately one-third of their clientele is involved in at least one point of entry or exit to secondary services alone. The extent of the information soon outstrips a conventional two-dimensional spreadsheet and recourse must be made to a multi-dimensional database.

With no custom-built software on the commercial market when fund-holding began, most practices developed their own recording methods in parallel to the fundholding software and moved from spreadsheets such as Excel to databases such as DB4 and Access to cope with the complexity of the expanding information. Many realized that the scope of fundholding might well expand and against all advice recorded in 'black-hole' fashion charting 'anything that moved'. Such black-hole recording is now proving invaluable to compare fundholding with non-fund-holding activities and a potential source of needs assessment information for Health Authorities and providers, whose information technology has not been up to the task, as well as information progress towards a practice's ability to purchase total care. These data have never been available before and are as yet not collected at local, let alone national level.

## Involving the partners

By the same token the volume and scope of a practice's activity are often such that it is beyond the ability of a fund manager from a clinical point of view or a GP from a management point of view to cope with them at all. Many practices have devolved the management, budget and under-standing of a specialty field to a specific partner. This has the added bonus of genuinely involving all the partners in the purchasing or com-missioning process. It allows that partner to become expert in the organ-ization and reorganization of his respective department(s) and to strike up special relationships with the provider trust's specialists and mana-gers concerned in secondary, community and social care. He or she will be familiar with his partners' and staff's referral patterns to his depart-ments, the waiting lists and the pattern of service provision from the providers.

'Ownership' and therefore informed responsibility and accountability is the most powerful lever for success. The responsible partner becomes a mine of resource information for his colleagues in terms of appoint-ment opportunities, matters of urgency and complaints, and by lateral thinking, a facilitator for change capable of strategic overview directly with provider trusts and Health Authorities alike. Striving for success becomes an issue of personal pride.

The division of labour must be clear and the communication between the partners explicit and maintained, otherwise such division of function will lead to chaos. It has the advantage of including partners reluctant to become involved in the overall panoply of fundholding and purchasing. By handling something they may at least enjoy they will be encouraged to take an interest in and form an allegiance with practice protocols and strategies. They may not feel that they are the only ones doing all the clinical work whilst their fundholding colleagues play about with the business side of the scheme.

## Monitoring performance and referral patterns

As well as the fund manager, all partners need substance behind verbal or hearsay reports. The database provides a snapshot of what is in the pipeline, the backlog of indebtedness and a starting point for prospective routine monitoring. Useful figures are:

1  *Referrals* – The number per month = referral rate.

2 *First consultations* – The number per month = the 'first seen' rate.

The difference between (1) and (2) in numbers is the amount by which the backlog is increasing/decreasing (plus or minus cost accrual) (*see* figure 12.2a).

The difference between an item progressing from (1) to (2) in dates is the waiting time for a consultation.

3 *Waiting list* – The number put on a waiting list per month = the waiting list rate.

The difference between (2) and (3) in numbers equals the 'strike rate conversion' (*see* figure 12.2b) which will vary from partner to partner depending on the personal idiosyncrasies of their referral habits and those of the specialists to whom they refer (see figure 12.2c).

4 *Operations* – The number of operations done per month = the 'op done' rate. This may vary with provider capacity or the degree to which the practice actively manages its own waiting list, a habit to be recommended.

The difference between (3) and (4) in numbers demonstrates the increase or decrease in backlog and cost accrual expenditure. The difference between an item progressing from (3) to (4) in dates is the waiting time for an operation. By addition averages and means may be calculated.

The difference between an item progressing from (1) to (4) is the overall waiting time, perhaps the most sensitive and realistic measurement of the true meaning of waiting.

5 *Follow-ups* – The number of follow-ups per month = the follow-up rate, which again may vary according to provider habit or purchaser contracting and allows for the calculation of numbers and costs waiting for follow-up.

The difference between (2) or (4) and (5) (consultations, operations and follow-ups) in numbers allows speculation and action for appropriate contracting and protocols.

# Internal audit

Suitable graphic print-outs from the database will establish easily understood patterns which can themselves lead to levers for change after audit and point the practice towards alterations of policy or protocols.

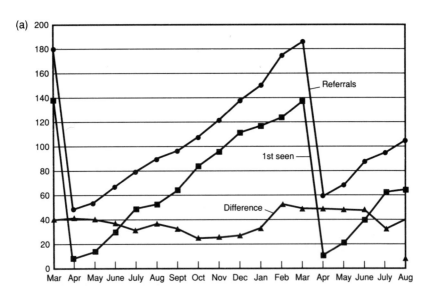

ENT referrals compared to first consultations resulting. Note little alterations
in pattern/running backlog

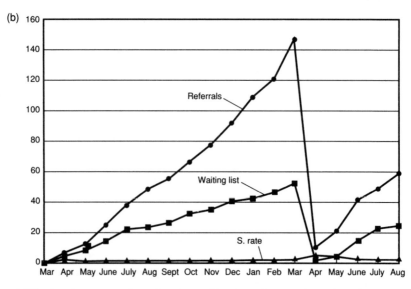

ENT referrals compared to referrals resulting in a place on the waiting list,
ie strike rate. Conversion steady at approximately 2:1 – satisfactory

**Figure 12.2** Lovemead Group Practice: Statistics for ENT, March 1993 to
August 1994, giving 'at a glance comparisons' of yearly statistics, year end and
overall development.

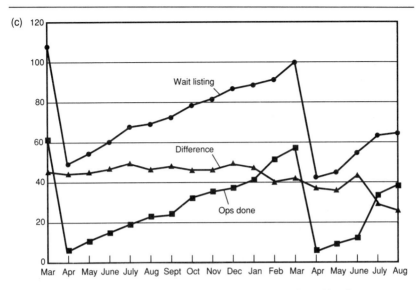

ENT waiting list compared to operations done. Reduction in waiting list backlog is apparent

Figure 12.2 *cont.*

Every practice activity carries a potential cost, real in the terms of activity within the fundholding scheme and notional if it devolves to the Health Authorities. All partners should have a basic understanding of the fundholding reports and schedules and be suitably tutored to a minimum understanding of the fundholding accounts. It would be an unusual practice that had partners uninterested in savings or the cost-effective use of staff. Fund or activity reports, whether they come from a database or modification of the fundholding software, provide the basis for regular practice meetings and the all-important comparison of business plan to out-turn reports and so performance management. This is the ammunition with which to face the Family Health Services Authority (FHSA), RHA (NHS Executive outposts from 1996) and, together with suitable tranquillization, fund managers to face the Audit Commission and on which to base estimates of health gain.

The raw data from these sources together with Prescription Analysis CosT (PACT) figures from the Prescription Pricing Authority (PPA) provide ample scope for the highlighting of areas to address for change or of dissatisfaction either as a result of provider inadequacies, partners' referral and prescribing habits, shortage of resources or simply to check providers' performance against contracts to ensure agreements are being met.

Fundholders would be well advised to keep a sharp eye on the commercial market as the humble origins of several practices' recording have now been developed commercially, some as add-on updates to fundholding software and some as stand-alone systems.

## Comparative performance monitoring

It is fair to add here a caveat. One of the aims of the reforms is to readjust the balance of care between the secondary and primary sectors so that care is delivered in the most appropriate place by the most appropriate providers. Primary care performance data currently suffer in this respect because there are as yet no agreed measures of performance or quality to inform such investment decisions.

Without hard qualitative performance indicators we have to rely on normative standards, i.e. how we differ from others doing the same thing. Whilst we may be able to show a change in performance by comparing year-on-year figures within a practice let us say, these are only relative to the mean of other practices. We are familiar with such normative comparisons as prescribing data from the PPA (above or below FHSA average, etc.) and where our practice may lie within a range of neighbouring practices referring to hospital departments from figures provided by the FHSA. However, it is impossible to know if practices on the extremes away from the mean are in fact providing appropriate or inappropriate, let alone cost-effective, care.

Attempts have been made to quantify quality such as the concept of QALYS (quality adjusted life years), but these are not easily applied to much of the 'softer' nature of many of the facets of primary care delivery. It may be relatively easy to measure and so compare the healing rate of leg ulcers, but is physiotherapy delivered in-house 'better' than the same physiotherapy at a hospital, or for the sake of argument how do you cost compassion? The objective measurement and cost evaluation of health gain within primary care itself or as a result of transfer to secondary care, remains an enigma. For some while yet we may have to rely on the subjective and wholly unsatisfactory measurement of patient satisfaction.

## Primary health care team integration

Primary care-led purchasing is coming to be acknowledged as the best available means of assessing and so delivering the health needs of the population. The responsibility for the delivery of practice-based primary care services should be devolved to the extended PHCT, no longer just the GP. It is therefore important that the PHCT is well developed, its members well trained and fully integrated into the practice and the population they serve.

This integration can be a slow process as old habits die hard. Many GPs are still unaware of the roles and functions carried out by some members of the PHCT, in particular health visitors and school nurses. With the arrival of the reforms many community nurses felt threatened and marginalized. However, many have since found that the reforms have brought a new awareness and recognition of their roles and responsibilities from GPs and managers. A spirit of genuine co-operation is beginning to develop between the professions.

Not only is it important to recruit the right staff but continuous effort must be made to ensure the team works as a team and not a collection of individuals. To plan, implement, monitor and manage change success-fully, teams must learn to trust fellow members, agree to agree and agree to differ while still continuing to function towards defined common goals. The team is more likely to be more successful if it can emphasize indi-vidual strengths and support individual weaknesses. It should be informed by good communications under effective discipline, all in the spirit of good humour. This is a tall order but achievable, if as much effort goes into team building as is used in the pursuit of aims and objectives.

To be fully effective to match these ideals a variety of roles within the team should be filled:

- leader
- thinker/creator
- doer/worker
- uniter/healer
- analyst/obsessional.

Whilst large teams may have a spread of personalities covering these headings a small team may be just as successful if some members fulfil more than one role. There are now many tutors available on the subject, ranging from professional management facilitators to distant learning projects, to which any PHCT could do well to subscribe. Performance management is a relatively new concept to GPs and health professionals, as well as some managers. Measuring the team performance against its objectives and active management (audit, by another name) whilst the team undertakes its allotted tasks is again as important as the task itself. Performance appraisal, from which to agree plans for building on the strengths and eliminating the weaknesses of individuals, with their hopes and ambitions for the future, completes the cycle, reinforcing the motivation and morale to move ahead.

All Health Service disciplines are now required to address targets, state objectives and perform against them, from *Health of the Nation*, the planning of savings, the addressing of 'charters', to fulfilling the aims of *Testing the Vision* (nurses) and *Changing Childbirth* (midwives). For many of us accustomed to just 'doing the job' in splendid isolation, this necessity to enquire 'what job am I doing?', 'how may I do it better?', 'who can help me?' and 'who can I help?', is a new discipline. The responsibility fundholders have for spending huge sums of taxpayers' money appropriately as well as doctoring makes the discipline and so the accountability both inevitable and obligatory – and extraordinarily satisfying.

13 Achievements of Fundholders

*Rhidian Morris*

In trying to describe the achievements of fundholding we should first understand where the development of general practice had reached at the time the present reforms were introduced.

In Britain there has been a long tradition of medical generalists (GPs) and medical specialists (consultants). When the NHS was created in 1948 the entire population was allocated to GPs' lists. Patients were required to see the GP first before they could be referred on to a specialist. However, it was to be 35 years before the gatekeeper role of the GP was properly recognized and described. This role was crucial to the development of the NHS and is now crucial to the development of health care world wide.

In 1948 general practice consisted of doctors working alone or in small groups working from simple premises that only opened for surgeries. There were no appointment systems and very few staff. The GP reacted to demand on a day-to-day basis. General practice responds to three types of pressure and then develops:

- financial pressure
- work-load
- professional pride.

All of these pressures can be demonstrated at various times in the NHS. Initially GPs responded to work-load by moving towards group practices, sharing work-load and providing cover for each other for sickness, holidays and out-of-hours work.

In 1966 the GP Charter was introduced. This was an enabling system. It encouraged GPs to work together, to employ staff and to improve their premises. Initially development was slow. There were, however, strong financial inducements in the 1966 Charter which encouraged the employment of staff and the provision of a range of services. Two other developments provided impetus to change. The development of health centres showed that properly staffed, attractive buildings were preferred by patients and also that health professionals working from the same building were more likely to develop a team spirit. When a sufficient number of practices are working from good premises and with good staff, other doctors move in that direction both for professional pride and because of a fear of loss of income if patients are attracted to better houses and better organized practices. The development of training practices and the introduction of compulsory training for general practice resulted in increasing medical standards within general practice. The new GP was being trained to deliver a wide range of services from good premises (Table 13.1).

**Table 13.1** The development of a modern GP

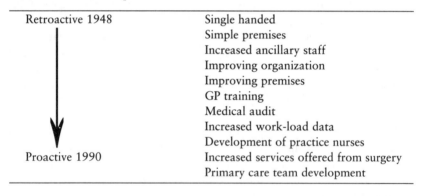

| Retroactive 1948 | Single handed |
| | Simple premises |
| | Increased ancillary staff |
| | Improving organization |
| | Improving premises |
| | GP training |
| | Medical audit |
| | Increased work-load data |
| | Development of practice nurses |
| Proactive 1990 | Increased services offered from surgery |
| | Primary care team development |

Those years saw general practice moving from a retroactive stance to a proactive stance. The greatest change occurred in the 1980s and by 1990 the profession was ready for a change. The Royal College of General Practitioners (RCGP) has often been accused of interfering too much in the 1980s. In reality it recognized the need for change and the potential that existed in general practice. However, it is largely an academic body and it approaches life from that viewpoint. It can be criticized for being weak on management and its approach was often naive. It placed too much emphasis on doing certain things without explaining why they were necessary, what management was required or how the GP could deliver without being overwhelmed with work. It continually called for the reduction of list size without recognizing the cost to the country of that policy. Nevertheless, it will play a vital role in the future on standards of care in general practice.

By 1990 many GPs possessed the following qualities:

- caring
- competitive
- organized
- good negotiator
- possessing good information
- proactive.

It is sad that very few people recognized that GPs were like this so that when fundholding was announced there were cries that GPs were not competent to manage the budget or to plan the health care of their patients. It was thought that the budget would interfere with the doctor–patient relationship. No one seemed to recognize that the GP was daily making rationing decisions in his gatekeeper role. The mistakes by NHS managers and planners were ignored.

Above all there was a failure to recognize that fundholding, like the 1966 Charter, was an enabling system and not a financially constricting system. Evidence from around the world suggests that the most cost-effective health care systems are those which have well developed primary care systems which act as gatekeepers. Extreme examples are Britain which spends 6.5% of GDP to provide good (excellent?) health care to 100% of its population, and the USA which spends 13% of GDP and does not cover 30% of its population for health care. In the USA, with a poorly developed primary care system, it is said that Ford spends more on health care for its employees than it does on buying steel for its cars.

Anything that improves the gatekeeping capability of primary care will improve the quality of care and allow a greater range of services to be offered for the same money. Fundholding offers a financial framework to collect data. That financial framework also means that providers must take notice of what the GP says and allows the GP to change the service offered, according to local circumstances. It is truly an enabling system, empowering the GP to tailor the NHS to the needs of his particular patients. It is a successor to the 1966 Charter but is as yet incomplete for the present GP contract does not allow the fundholder complete flexibility in how he delivers health care.

So has fundholding actually achieved anything or is it a different way of delivering exactly the same as before?

The original criticisms of fundholding can be dismissed. Fundholders have proved remarkably able financial administrators, creating savings whilst decreasing waiting lists and providing a wider range of services. They have proved more flexible planners than the old NHS planners. Rod Smith of Reading has ably demonstrated the extraordinary inequity of orthopaedic consultant cover that existed in Oxfordshire. Fundholders are correcting that and the DHAs are following. Far from fundholding ruining the doctor–patient relationship, it appears to have strengthened it with no evidence of lists dropping but the reverse happening and the patient grateful for the fundholder's ability to act on their behalf.

Whilst the 1966 Charter was an enabling system it did actually restrict what GPs could do. This led to frustration amongst many GPs. In 1994 a survey was undertaken of National Association of Fundholding Practices (NAFP) members to assess innovations in fundholding practices due solely to fundholding. That survey is not yet complete but the first 100 replies gave this response:

- waiting list initiative            49%
- new staff                          59%
- in-house out-patients              43%
- in-house services                  84%
- completely new services            33%
- alliances with others              44%
- new audits                         28%
- new monitoring systems             32%
- use of private sector              56%
- changes in community services      23%
- improved relationships with DHA    22%
- reduced waiting lists              21%

The list of in-house services was impressive and included the following:

| | | |
|---|---|---|
| Ultra-sound | Counsellor | Audiology |
| Orthopaedic | Rheumatology | Stress management |
| Chiropody | Vasectomy | Yoga |
| Pain clinic | Physiotherapy | Psychologist |
| Acupuncture | Speech therapy | Osteopathy |
| Nurse management | Sigmoidoscopy | Surgical O/P |

| | | |
|---|---|---|
| Dietitian | Community psychiatric | ECG |
| Gynaecology | nursing | Endoscopy |
| Urology | Minor Ops | Cryo-surgery |
| Dermatology | Ophthalmology | Day-case surgery |
| Investigations | Complementary medicine | Phlebotomist |
| Geriatrics | Cardiology | |

This list is not complete. It appears that every type of out-patient apart from regional specialties – e.g. renal, neuro-surgery, plastic surgery – has occurred somewhere.

There is a wide range of new services that were previously unavailable to individual practices including much of the previous list. It appears our NHS provided a multi-tier service with large variations in services offered to the patient in the community. It is difficult to think of any other system which would have created such large-scale change so quickly and amazingly with so little disruption to the NHS. We are witnessing a revolution in primary care. A revolution driven by GPs. True primary care teams are being created. A wider range of services is being offered more quickly and more conveniently to patients.

The practices themselves have changed. Maggie Marum in her position as Fundholding Lead Officer for the South-West RHA surveyed practices to see what effect fundholding had on the management of practices. She found changes occurring with greater analysis of what the practice was doing and achieving. She also identified training needs as practices adapted and looked for help in achieving new skills. These practices are developing a more scientific approach to health care, analysing, experimenting, adapting. Those of us who have undergone this change realize just how different we are since 1990.

## Relationships

Primary care was a black hole as far as RHAs were concerned. What contact there was, tended to be through a few academic GPs. Fund-holding thrust the RHAs into daily contact with GPs. The learning curve was steep and for many fundholders their relationship with the Regions was closer than with the Family Health Services Authorities (FHSAs). A genuine bond has been created. Fundholders are strident in their demands that when Regional Executive Outposts are created in 1996 they will retain responsibility for fundholding and that a right of appeal to the Region on fundholding issues will remain. This bond is important for it has taught the Regions that the bulk of medical care occurs in primary care and that there is enormous potential for development. Medical care must be looked at in its entirety. It must be viewed flexibly, not inflexibly and compartmentalized. The Regional Outposts are well placed to feed back a lot of information to fundholders to improve their databases and therefore their decision making. The method of communication with fundholders in the Regions has moved away from meetings of all fundholders for the numbers are too great, but instead towards meetings of Regional fundholders' representatives, sometimes elected by fundholders, sometimes appointed by Regions. Some Regions have written contracts with their fundholders. These links will become more important when Regions become NHS Executive Outposts.

Relationships with FHSA have significantly changed. For the first time FHSAs were faced with two different systems. The fundholder has greater independence than the non-fundholder. He has a responsibility for assessing need and delivering health care that is arguably greater than that of the FHSA for his legal responsibility is personal and not corporate. FHSAs changed in response to developing greater knowledge of health needs assessment, of audit and secondary care. Recognizing that it was increasingly difficult to separate primary from secondary care, FHSAs started collaborating with DHAs. Then a few effectively merged and in 1996 all will probably have merged. This is probably a direct consequence of fundholding which has proved the feasibility of assessing health needs as a whole and not divided into secondary and primary care.

Relationships with DHAs vary considerably. There are many examples of close collaboration, e.g. Dorset Health Commission or Plymouth and Torbay Health Authorities. In those cases where DHAs ignored fundholders they have been forced to talk to them simply because of the changes they have created. Some have argued that the purchaser/provider split would not have worked without the catalytic effect of fundholding and it is difficult to disagree. Fundholding brought DHAs a knowledge of primary care, a recognition of the need to work with FHSAs and a growing recognition that it is impossible to purchase effectively without consulting GPs. DHAs have also learned the need for flexible and enforceable contracts and also the need for doctor input into contracts. They have been shown that there are different ways of delivering health care and that the established way of delivering secondary care might have been moving in the wrong direction. Fundholders have almost made different creatures out of DHAs. The relationship is fascinating for they need each other. The DHA with its power, its

Director of Public Health and its planning ability, needs the fundholding flexibility, knowledge and closeness to patients, and vice versa. They actually compete for resources and contracts, but need each other. A state of creative tension exists between the two which can only result in innovation.

The Primary Care Division of the NHS Executive has been altered by its responsibility for fundholding for it is now significantly affecting the way secondary care is delivered. That could alter its role within the Executive. Fundholders would be foolish not to recognize the knowledge the Executive has now gained about primary care and about GPs themselves. Fundholding has given them intimate knowledge of general practice and our representative bodies would do well to recognize that.

The realization that if a fundholder refers his patients elsewhere income to the hospital will fall has had a dramatic effect on hospitals. It is not just the old joke that consultants have started sending GPs Christmas cards. Hospitals now have Fundholding Officers who liaise with fundholders and many have Primary Care Liaison Officers who talk to all the GPs in their catchment areas. Waiting lists have dwindled as GPs using cost-per-case and cost and volume contracts have insisted that quality conditions are met. Fundholders have been more successful than DHAs in achieving shorter waiting lists and in many cases improved the quality of the service. Many fundholders also have regular meetings with consultants and this is an effective method of easing change. The success of fundholders in reducing waiting lists has given rise to the accusation of two tiers. Have we ever known a success accused like this before? Would people cry 'two tiers' if someone introduced better treatments? No, they would switch to the new treatment. Why are DHAs not castigated if they do not match fundholders' achievements and why is it that when they do somone says there is no need for fundholding? We cannot leave hospitals without referring to consultants doing clinics in GPs' surgeries. This is a significant trend that not only provides care more conveniently for patients but challenges the role that modern hospitals play. Do they really need to be so large? Is there not an argument for smaller high-technology central hospitals with peripheral cottage-type hospitals providing out-patient and non-major surgery?

Community nursing is in the process of being transformed by fundholders. In the 1980s Nurse Managers concentrated on locality nursing instead of practice-based nursing. Attempts to create a primary care team spirit were thwarted by the nurses' need to look to their managers. In effect this proud profession was actually being de-professionalized. Fundholders are insisting on practice-based nurses working within the team in a flexible manner. They look for nurses who are independent and who can initiate change. In other words, professionals. The development of practice nurses in the 1980s was a success story. The development of community nurses will be worth watching. With more and more hospital procedures being carried out as day cases or actually in the community, greater skills will be required. How soon will nurse practitioners be amongst us? These changes are beginning to happen in fundholding practices and it is in these practices that future change is likely to occur. At last a true primary health care team is developing.

The growth of physiotherapy in fundholding practices has been phenomenal. Dietitians are also appearing in practices where there were none, and where fundholders spearhead, non-fundholders follow.

There have been several interesting experiments where fundholding practices work closely with Social Services. Methods vary from having an attached social worker to having an attached care manager, to having a formal working arrangement with Social Services. After 40 years of poor relationships, fundholders are moving towards closer working relationships because having accepted responsibility for delivering health care they recognize the necessity of a good relationship with Social Services.

Fundholders were initially regarded as outcasts by some sections of the medical profession. As a result they created their own representative body, the National Association of Fundholding Practices (NAFP). Relationships between the NAFP and other bodies are in their infancy but it is possible to describe the following scenario.

- *GMSC* – The Trade Union section of representation negotiating on pay and terms of service and responding to proposals from the NHS Executive.

- *RCGP* – The academic body involving itself with standards of medical care, training and research.

- *NAFP* – Involving itself in developing health care systems. In effect the practical side of medicine that GPs are good at. How do you get health care to the patient? Developing management systems. Involving itself at a very early stage with interested bodies in the development of ideas. Increasing the involvement of Primary Care Managers.

These three roles are distinctive but there are bound to be overlapping responsibilities. At the time of writing, there are signs that the BMA and GMSC are beginning to accept fundholding. If they do not they cannot expect to go on representing fundholders even in their salary negotiations. There is a chance of a very creative relationship between these three organizations. Let us hope it is not missed.

We are witnessing a revolution in health care in this country. Fund-holding is at the forefront of that revolution. Relationships between GPs and other sections of the NHS have changed. Arguably, the structure of the NHS has changed because of fundholding. The services offered and the sites of delivery are changing. Our concepts of hospital care may alter as almost certainly will the relationships between consultants and the primary care team. Far from having left behind a golden age of general practice, we are moving towards one. Changes are required to our GMS contract to allow the flexible approach to delivering health care that will be required. Whilst the NAFP will play a powerful role in these changes, never has there been such a need for the negotiating powers of the GMSC on pay and terms of service or the academic abilities of the RCGP in ensuring that standards of care are high.

In a world of limited resources but ever-increasing medical capabilities at escalating prices, it is inevitable that all countries will seek value for money in health care. We must accept this and pick up the challenge. For doctors the choice is clear. Manage the care of your patients in a cost-effective manner or be managed yourself by others. Is state *controlled* medicine with all its dangers really an option we can allow to happen? We must manage ourselves for no one is better placed or motivated to act in the patients' best interests.

Fundholding can claim the following achievements.

- Greater equity of service delivered in primary care.

- Greater range of services delivered more conveniently for the patients.

- A more flexible and quicker response to patients' needs.

- Shorter waiting lists.

- Greater management expertise in primary care.

- The creation of true primary care health teams.

- More flexible and effective use of community nurses.

- Closer working relationships with Regions, Districts and FHSAs.

- Greater use of audit.

It is only 3 years since fundholding was introduced. The rate of change is phenomenal. The achievements are great and yet commentators are still looking for every excuse to castigate fundholding and look for its destruction. Truth eventually emerges and British general practice cannot allow the opportunities offered by fundholding to slip from its grasp.

14 Representing Fundholders

*Malcolm Fox*

The purpose of this chapter is to examine the various ways in which fundholders are being represented and to look at the effectiveness of the process. It is therefore interesting to look at how these processes have developed to gain some understanding of their relative importance.

1989 heralded the biggest upheaval to general practice in the UK since 1948, the first feature being the presentation by Government of a proposed new contract and the second being the publication of the Government's proposals to reform the NHS, including the initial outlines for GP fundholding.

The overall response of GPs to the new contract was one of dismay and almost instinctive rejection, which dominated practitioners' thoughts and discussion and monopolized traditional medical politics. Against this background the fundholding proposal was rejected by the majority with little rational discussion taking place. Within a short period it was obvious that only a few practices and practitioners were keen to take up the offer and in doing so they would be isolated from colleagues and subjected to quite abusive attacks on their honesty and motivation. This immediately resulted in the breaking down of many traditional networks of mutual support and assistance.

As the full extent of the changes throughout the Health Service became more obvious it became apparent that the new Family Health Services Authorities (FHSAs), replacing the old Family Practitioner Committees, were in a state of flux almost amounting to chaos. New senior staff were being appointed and staff at all levels were having to prepare for radically different roles and procedures. In this position the potential fundholders felt lonely and anxious. The level of intra-professional abuse was such that many felt unable to make their position public and they were forced to gradually develop new support and representation networks. Simultaneously new players began to be apparent, the most obvious being the RHA, with some form of primary care unit frequently staffed by personnel with little in-depth knowledge of general practice. The information and guidance being made available from the NHS Management Executive (ME) and the Department of Health was minimal and often inadequately developed.

This heady mixture of threat, abuse and ignorance against a background of a new and fascinating challenge to GPs, with a very clear national political will to see the proposed changes implemented, inevitably forced practices to develop entirely new styles and methods of external relationships. These new relationships set the tone and style for the future of fundholding representation.

## Liaising with local fundholders

The first stirring of both formal and informal representation of fundholders began from local groupings. All organizations have their strengths and weaknesses and the common problem is the absence of skills and resources. Many individual practices found themselves lacking sufficient resources and self-confidence to cope with all the changes involved in fundholding. The meeting together of local practices proved mutually supportive and promoted self-confidence and good morale. The practicability of this process varied with many factors. Geographically isolated practices had particular difficulties, which they shared with others in Districts where only one or two opted into the scheme.

A barrier to the development of effective local relations between practices is the existence of competition but this can be overcome by an emphasis on common shared problems. The exchange at this level of advice, explanation and experience is to the benefit of individual practices and facilitates speedy movement up the learning curve. Despite anxieties these local liaison arrangements have not interfered with practices' ability to manage their own affairs as privately as they wish. The representation of practices in local meetings by a mixture of GPs and their managers facilitated liaison on a wide range of issues.

Once the concept of local liaison is accepted and begins to function in a supportive and educational role then the group can develop further. Obviously this can be at a formal level and become some form of consortium. This aspect is covered elsewhere but many advantages can be advanced for putting a great deal of effort into local inter-practice relationships without proceeding as far as formal consortium formation. These can be listed:

• pooling and checking data

- sharing of knowledge of the provider market

- developing contract monitoring

- preparation of common contract outlines

- sharing contracts

- jointly bidding for funds, e.g. waiting-list initiatives

- developing or influencing training for fundholding

- public relations

- various degrees of joint contract negotiation

- develop common policies on the use of savings

- jointly encourage provider innovation by 'pump priming' with savings.

The reasons for wishing to do any or all of these things jointly will vary from group to group and from practice to practice. Some are done to maximize the use of a scarce resource such as personnel or time. At other times the driving force will be the lack of sufficiently robust information from any one practice in any single area or to maximize impact by aggregating money and numbers.

The joint negotiation of contracts by local associations of fundholders can initially appear to challenge a fundamental tenet of the system, which is the ability to negotiate flexible local arrangements which are practice sensitive. In reality local fundholding purchasers will often have common objectives in terms of type of service and can mutually reinforce their negotiating position, leaving final details such as volume and contract type to individual practices. Similarly, commonly developed contracting documents can smooth administrative processes at both the purchaser and provider base. Such common documents will also facilitate joint contract monitoring.

The development of trusting relationships between local fundholders allowing a fair amount of joint activity but retaining the final level of decision within the practice will reinforce their ability to influence the development of the system.

Local groups of fundholding practices co-operating together, often channelled through individual representatives, form an ideal functional link with other local purchasing authorities and consortia. Such links can be used for mutual education, information exchange and even joint purchasing.

# The RHA link

The first new link made by fundholders to a formal body outside the normal area of practice activity is to the RHA. As the initial major roles of the RHA with regard to fundholding are in vetting the suitability of applicant practices and in setting budgets, practices need to learn how to represent themselves in a positive and organized manner.

This will probably mean that representation of the practice is delegated to one or two partners and the practice managerial staff. Jointly they need to understand the managerial culture of business meetings with prepared agendas, marshalled information and the need to agree outcome and activity. They need to be prepared to meet personnel whose detailed understanding of the business of general practice may be limited and who may need a great deal of explanation. This will certainly be combined with extensive knowledge of the secondary care sector and a high level of intellectual inquisitiveness and learning capacity. To represent their practices adequately the individuals will need to combine the best clinical consultation skills with the sort of preparation previously put into viva examinations. The clinician thus armed is a good match for most managers and will represent his or her practice well.

The preparation in written form of information and opinion of an individual practice is justified and is often used at this level. This process helps to clarify thought and can be facilitated by practice management staff and simple technology of the word-processing type. Representation of individual practices by written communications and plans will probably increase in importance as the number of Regions is contracted and more processes are conducted at a distance.

The second area of representing practices with Regions is in the negotiation of budgets, unless this has been delegated to FHSAs. In general the same principles and skills are essential. The practice objective needs to be determined in advance, information prepared and presented and the practice interests advocated carefully and positively.

As the number of fundholding practices grows and as the number of Regions decreases it will be increasingly difficult to represent or even gain audience for individual practice representation at this level. The need to do so will continue and possibly even increase as broad strategic directions will be set at this level. The Department of Health may devolve a greater range of activities to this level including local negotiation of primary care contracts and pay. The extent and nature of fundholding is going to develop and change, and informed representation from operational levels should be integral to the process. To cope with these changes the local groupings of fundholders need to jointly develop representation at Regional level. This can take the form of a Regional branch of the National Association of Fundholding Practices (NAFP) or some more local sub-division. The aversion of present central Government to organizations acting in any way which can be termed a Trade Union indicates that looser groupings may be more acceptable.

## The FHSA link

The fundholding practice has to develop a whole new range of relationships with the FHSA. These will be most obvious in the financial and planning areas.

The two major functions of the FHSA of settling financial accounts for fundholders and the organization of the auditing of the yearly accounts are probably the areas demanding the greatest accuracy and attention to detail by the practice. There is a need to present clear and accurate detail, well authenticated and with an understanding of the restraints on the FHSA for probity and statutory obligations.

Where Regional functions such as budget allocation for some or all of the fund and monitoring of planning are delegated to the FHSA, the individual practice will necessarily represent itself. More strategic decisions by the FHSA on underlying principles or policies may well necessitate joint negotiation with other practices. Again this is an area where the local or locality group of practices is necessary to develop local consensus without necessitating total conformity of view. The regular presence of an FHSA officer at local meetings can be very useful in facilitating mutual education and co-operation.

The individual practice's relationship with the FHSA or its successor body such as Health Commissions (HCs), is inevitably different from that with the RHA because of the former's involvement in the core business of practices in delivering primary care. Rightly the FHSA will be seeking reassurance that the fundholding element of practice activity is not performed in a manner which can result in a poorer general practice. To meet this continuing obligation the practice will need to explain the whole of its services and their interrelationships and outcomes, usually described in the annual business plan. Where savings from the fund are spent in more traditional areas of practice then its representatives will need to be explicit and accurate to avoid any impression of deception.

## Linking with purchasing bodies

Gradually already, and shortly formally, the FHSAs are being merged with purchasing DHAs. The new bodies have a variety of titles, usually including the term commissioning. The presence of officers from these bodies at meetings of local groupings of fundholders facilitates co-operation and allows a channel of informal representation.

Simultaneously these joint authorities are developing methods of communication with local practitioners by various combinations of locality management and GP representation, frequently on a paid basis, some of whom should be of a fundholder background. The primary care medical advisers employed by Authorities additionally form further channels open to individual fundholding practices and local groupings to influence the Authorities.

## The role of the Local Medical Committee

The Local Medical Committee (LMC) in its statutory role has always had the responsibility of representing all practitioners with the FHSA. In reality the medico-political aspect of the LMC's activities and the majority rejection of fundholding has resulted in abandonment of this task with regard to fundholders. This has been a variable picture throughout the country, where in some instances affected practices and/or practitioners have ceased all contact with their LMC and in other areas where either individual fundholders or even considerable numbers have continued to take part in LMC activities.

The ever-growing extent of fundholding and the mainstream adoption of the primary care role in purchasing with its various locality-type schemes are changing attitudes. The LMC structures now recognize the need to represent all types of practices if only because they will be gradually sidelined if they do not do so. This pragmatism can still be a thin veneer on top of innate and often political antagonism with the result that the LMC activity on behalf of fundholders is not likely to be particularly vigorous.

Despite these problems the representatives at the Annual Conference of LMCs have moved to a position where they have withdrawn their outright rejection of fundholding. This has been effected by a wish at the LMCs to hold the profession together and heal the wounds. At this level the original abusive accusations against fundholders of greed and neglecting patients' interests have become more muted.

As fundholding becomes the norm, especially if accompanied by some new form of primary care contracting, the LMC structure will have to change radically or it will become increasingly archaic and irrelevant.

# The representation of fundholders by General Medical Services Committee (GMSC)

The initial immediate rejection of the fundholding concept by GMSC and its encouragement of a vituperative anti-reform policy inevitably resulted in the majority of potential fundholders believing that the GMSC was unwilling to represent them in any form. The fact that fundholders shared the same problems as most other practices in responding to the new contract was ignored, as was the fact that a number of medical politicians saw the system as one which empowered general practice.

A small number of GMSC members known to be fundholders continued to be elected and entirely new members of the same persuasion appeared. Their advocacy, combined with the obvious early successes of fundholding in breaking many local log-jams in services, began to have an effect in changing opinions. From the first stages GMSC stated that all practitioners contributed to its activity and should be represented. This was initially 'tokenistic' but there was anxiety that a division of real depth would occur, resulting in the sort of problems that had previously occurred when junior doctors and breakaway groups of consultants had left the BMA in the past. The GMSC recognized that Government saw it as a Trade Union but did not understand that many fundholders felt its activities appeared to be more Luddite than thoughtful.

The importance of the GP knowledge of patient need ensured that all purchasing organizations within the new structures began to seek out their views in a variety of ways. The power this gave to general practice was soon appreciated by GMSC. This did not sit easily with outright rejection of fundholding and the politically more acceptable term of 'commissioning of care' came to be used. This term was used to include fundholding and a formal sub-committee under this title was formed. Already the NAFP was in existence and was asked to nominate representatives to this body. This was obviously done to forestall any breakaway movement and to maintain GMSC credibility with Government as the nationally representative body.

The conflict between this pragmatism and the policy of both the conference of LMCs mandating GMSC, and that of the BMA was not sustainable in the long term. This resulted in the Chairman of GMSC proposing to the conference that it should modify its opposition to fundholding. A form of words was eventually agreed and in due course a fundholding sub-committee was formed.

This prolonged explanation may seem to be unnecessary, but it demonstrates how at last fundholders gained access to the GMSC's capabilities and facilities in areas such as terms of service, regulations and legal services with regard to fundholding, these activities being left initially to the NHS structures without necessarily protecting individual doctors and practices.

## BMA

The degree of separation of GMSC from the BMA is not easily understood but in reality GMSC is a body which represents all GPs via the Local Medical Committees (LMCs) with its separate finances raised by the LMC levies. The BMA represents any medical practitioner from any branch who has opted to join. Initially this separation was immaterial but as the GMSC stance has changed to a more pragmatic view of fundholding the tensions with the BMA continue to rise. Much of the consultant opposition to the empowerment of general practice is obvious within the BMA. There is also an increasing politicizing of BMA activity, and the adoption of party-political stances by prominent individual members. Therefore the practical ability of this body to represent fundholding in any form is negligible despite the public stance of wishing to represent all doctors in the UK.

## The NAFP

Once the offer of fundholding was made it was obvious that practices becoming involved would wish to discuss the project with other colleagues in the same position. The antagonism of existing organizations ensured that something separate was necessary. The pre-existing Conservative Medical Association might have appeared the inevitable focus of those with a political motivation but only seemed to attract a few.

Local loose groupings of those with fundholding interests showed a necessity to come together on a Regional basis in order to relate to the RHA. The development of a national body from these local groupings was a natural evolution ably assisted by a number of strong personalities who effectively articulated the advantages of fundholding in the public forum and simultaneously influenced the Department of Health over initial problems.

An interesting revolutionary feature of the organization was its acceptance of corporate practice membership and full membership of non-doctors in the form of both practice and NHS managers. The organization struggled initially with the problem as to whether its role was one of a special interest group or whether it should attempt to represent the doctors of fundholding practices for all purposes effectively in competition with GMSC. The initial policy has been one of a special interest group in which role it has been effective at national and Regional level in influencing events and policy. The question as to whether to evolve into a more general representative role is still not totally resolved.

## The National Association of Health Authorities and Trusts (NAHAT)

From its beginnings the NAFP developed a dialogue with NAHAT, eventually developing into a formalized associate membership. This has happened at a time when NAHAT has been internally in turmoil over personalities and the problem of how to represent the conflicting interests of purchasers and providers whom it generally saw as large organizations.

As the proportion of the population cared for by fundholders has grown and some fundholders are advocating an even greater range of services being included within the fund this is dynamizing a greater interest within the NAHAT. This should develop readily as there is much common ground in rationalizing cumbersome practical aspects of the scheme and clarifying roles and the regulations.

## What representation does fundholding need?

It could be said that the essence of fundholding is the total freedom of action of any involved practice to function as it sees best in the interests of its patients. In reality, with the large volumes of public money involved and the inevitable high profile of health in national politics, the process is going to be subjected to much enquiry and pressuring especially on accountability and change.

Therefore, fundholding needs to be represented by committed individuals involved in the process with an ability to understand both the minutiae and the grand strategy. Those representatives need to have excellent presentation and negotiation skills to advocate the advantages and needs of fundholding to an audience which extends from the public to professional colleagues and into the organizations of the Health Service, including the NHS Executive and the Department of Health. Any representatives need to have their origins in the practicalities of fundholding at practice level and the confidence and support of their colleagues.

15 Fundholding Consortia

## Peter Smith

*The mass of men lead lives of quiet desperation – except fund-holders (with apologies to Thoreau).*

The introduction of fundholding has undoubtedly proved to be the most significant change within general practice since the inception of the NHS. The mythology of the brave new world of fundholding abounds with tales of heroic deeds wrought by fundholders for the benefits of their patients. However, set against a background of scarce resources and less than universal acceptance of the scheme, one man's epic victory might well be perceived as another man's rout.

Differential delivery of primary care between practices has always been tolerated. The presence or absence of services within a particular practice has until recently depended upon the motivation and skills of the individual partners and the space available. Many GPs have found it less easy to accept the extension of this differential delivery to secondary care. Others have been deterred by the work that fundholding entails. A greater number still have insufficient patients to be eligible but fear that their practice population will be disadvantaged if they do not join the scheme (hence the quotation at the beginning of the chapter). Most of the latter group are wary of throwing in their lot with another practice without an independent, non-threatening system of supervision and arbitration.

Co-operative ventures were initially developed to offer the benefits of fundholding whilst addressing these basic difficulties.

The remainder of this chapter is divided into three parts. The first deals with the theoretical aspects of consortia; the second deals with the practical aspects and the third deals with possible future developments. I make no apologies for making references throughout to the Kingston and Richmond Multifund system developed jointly by Dr Jeremy Harris and myself. The same system has been adopted successfully in Kent, Birmingham, Eastleigh, Newham and many other areas.

# Part 1: The theory

## Definition

A *fundholding consortium is a group of two or more existing or prospective individual funds acting together in the management of their budgets.*

In this definition, I have excluded multipractice funds, since these constitute a single entity and therefore cannot form a consortium. The term 'acting together' is meant to imply active co-operation rather than agreement not to disadvantage one another. (Our own multifund also includes in the definition: 'pooling management allowances to employ high-quality staff to assist in the management of their budgets'.)

Excluded from this definition are any groups that do not consist exclusively of existing and/or prospective fundholders.

## The benefits of consortium fundholding

Forming a fundholding consortium should not be seen merely as a way of avoiding the possible unpleasant results of being left out of the scheme. There are positive benefits to working collectively. These include:

- access to secondary care remains similar across the consortium

- the work-load is minimized

- small practices can join and use the consortium management team as independent supervision.

Experience has shown that groups of GPs meeting thus extend the forum for co-operation and debate into areas well outside the boundaries of fundholding. Many feel that consortium fundholding offers the opportunity to influence the planning of local health services. Others see potential benefits in research and general practice development by sharing accurate information. In future, it is likely that consortia will take on added importance and other functions.

## Problems addressed by the consortium approach

### Differential delivery of care

At present, only 30% or so of the population is covered by fundholding. Patients outside the scheme are covered by DHA contracts which cannot be sensitive to the needs of individual practice populations. As *Health 2000* puts it, this is 'not money following patients, but patients following contracts'[1]. If all practices in a given area enter fundholding under the same banner, there is a greater likelihood that the benefits of the contract negotiation process will be shared by all.

GPs have their own good reasons for not joining the scheme. By addressing their fears (as we believe we have done in the multifund), they can be encouraged to join the commissioning process in consortia.

## Lack of strategic planning

As the number of fundholders in a given area increases, the collective impact of decisions made by individual GPs starts to affect *all* aspects of health care. Without a strategic view, shared with other health care commissioners, the planning of local health services eventually becomes impossible. Local providers, too, have to pay close attention to GP purchasers if they are to continue to receive referrals and hence funding to enable them to survive. The existence of a forum in the form of a consortium such as the multifund allows funds to discuss the strategic implications of their decisions.

## Involvement of providers

As the number of fundholders in a given area increases, it becomes more difficult for a provider to find the time to address the needs of each practice. The establishment of a core contract and a single channel of communication avoids duplication of negotiation and still allows the individual fund's voice to be heard where this differs from the collective view.

As the consortium system develops, there is no reason why providers and purchasers should not agree joint strategies for the development of local health services.

## The cost of singleton fundholding

Should all GPs in the country decide to go fundholding, the cost of the management allowance would become prohibitively expensive. Costs can be reduced considerably by combining to form consortia. Were the system to be extended, the dual systems of DHA and fundholder commissioning could be rationalized. For instance accurate needs assessment would be carried out by practices. This would reduce the need for the public health department to employ staff and information technology to carry out this function. Some existing staff could then be employed to assist funds in their commissioning role.

## The time spent by GPs on administration

The use of practice-based data entry clerks and area managers employed by the consortium allows GPs the benefits of fundholding without the excessive administrative burden. Practices should notice little disruption to practice life, and the management team should act on the fund's behalf in negotiation. The result is maximum involvement with minimal work.

## Suggested alternatives to fundholding do not give GPs any statutory function or rights within the commissioning process

A recent BMJ article purported to show a good alternative to fundholding[2]. Closer inspection of the figures shows that only 53% (70 out of 131) of the participating GPs were prepared to declare that the system was effective whilst the other 47% felt that they were not listened to. The reality is that, without statutory purchasing rights, GPs can only act as advisers.

## Patients have no input into commissioning of local services

'It is all too easy to forget that the purpose of the reforms is not organisational perfection but to improve people's health'[3]. *Health 2000* states that Labour would find 'a wider constituency to draw on than currently exists, for the creation of a health forum....The role of the CHC...is an area we will explore further'[1]. All major parties recognize the importance of local people 'owning' any plan for local health services. This does not mean a loss of commissioning power, but real sensitivity to local requirements.

# Part 2: Setting up a consortium

## Preparing the ground

Consider the potential conflicts of interests within a commissioning body that requires money to commission services, but may also have to recommend the amount that is top-sliced from this budget to go to the fundholders in the district. Remember also that the FHSA that is included in any future joint commissioning body is required to 'police' the activity of GPs.

Although many commissioning bodies have been admirably encouraging in the setting up of fundholding consortia, there is no doubt they should be organized and run by GPs. On the basis of our multifund experience, I would recommend that a *very* small group is responsible for preparing a local feasibility study, preferably consisting of only one or two local GPs. Avoid the temptation of having too many cooks. The broth requires speedy analysis, quick decision making and effective action if it is not to be spoilt in the preparation stage.

In Kingston and Richmond, all interested local GPs contributed £50 each to a central fund to pay for locum cover to allow Dr Harris and myself to spend a morning a week examining, among other things: possible management structures, obtaining information on available computers, preparing explanatory literature, looking for appropriate accommodation and pulling it all together to produce a final feasibility study.

The alternative approach is to hire experienced personnel on a consultancy basis. A consultancy team from the Kingston and Richmond Multifund could be hired, for instance, to assist in the practicalities of setting up a local structure. Having done this, a couple of local GPs should remain as medical managers to deal with the important medical aspects of contract negotiation.

Remuneration of medical managers is a vexed question, but is essential if GPs are to be encouraged to take on this type of non-GMS work. Working GPs, from their own experience, can ensure that the system responds to the needs of individual practices. Without their input, the consortium could easily drift towards becoming a traditional DHA-like structure. At present it is possible for medical managers to be paid as consultants to the consortium.

## The structure of the consortium (Figure 15.1)

When setting up a consortium, take account of the advice of the National Health Service Management Executive (NHSME), which was issued in the form of a circular in 1992. The basic thrust of the advice was:

- individual funds should both remain responsible for the use of their own budgets and accountable for the delivery of national and local objectives

- separate accounts should be kept with separate in-year financial monitoring for each fundholder

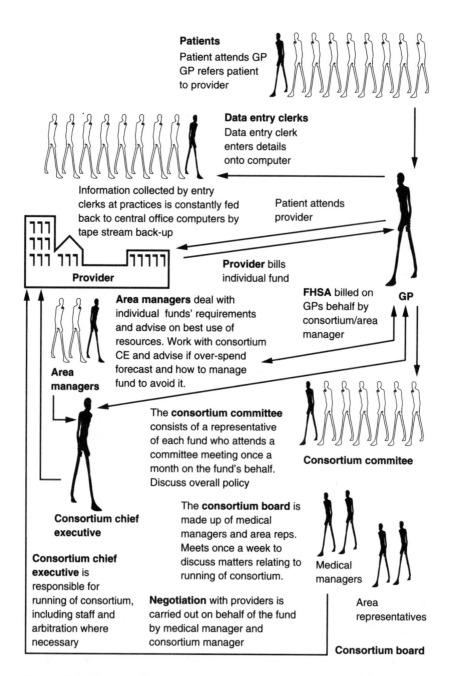

**Patients**
Patient attends GP
GP refers patient
to provider

**Data entry clerks**
Data entry clerk
enters details
onto computer

Information collected by entry
clerks at practices is constantly fed
back to central office computers by
tape stream back-up

Patient attends
provider

**Provider**

**Provider** bills
individual fund

**FHSA** billed on
GPs behalf by
consortium/area
manager

**GP**

**Area managers** deal with
individual funds' requirements
and advise on best use of
resources. Work with consortium
CE and advise if over-spend
forecast and how to manage
fund to avoid it.

**Area
managers**

The **consortium committee**
consists of a representative
of each fund who attends a
committee meeting once a
month on the fund's behalf.
Discuss overall policy

**Consortium commitee**

**Consortium chief
executive**

The **consortium board** is
made up of medical
managers and area reps.
Meets once a week to
discuss matters relating to
running of consortium.

**Consortium chief
executive** is
responsible for
running of consortium,
including staff and
arbitration where
necessary

**Negotiation** with providers is
carried out on behalf of the fund
by medical manager and
consortium manager

**Medical
managers**

**Area
representatives**

**Consortium board**

Figure 15.1 Diagram of consortium structure

- there should be agreed contingency arrangements to cover practices joining and leaving the consortium

- consortia should be able to offer economies of scale

- individual funds should have their own input into the contracting process, basing their choices on the needs of their practice population.

It is worth noting from the outset that the above advice also accords with the notion of the independent contractor status of the GP.

There are two areas alluded to that are difficult to address – accountability and economies of scale. The reference to 'local and national guidelines' has yet to be fully explored. Certainly, most GPs would be unhappy to join a voluntary scheme that is supposed to offer them greater freedom, only to be restricted by a planning system into which they at present have no statutory input.

The second area is 'economies of scale'. Most consortia will offer economies of scale on the management allowance and probably on computing. However, it could be argued that value for money would be a more appropriate term. A bulk order for computer hardware may be offered at a cheaper rate. It may well be more useful, however, to buy more powerful computers with modems, for instance, for the same price.

## Management structure

It is vital to keep the final structure simple. Lines of communication with obvious points of contact must be clear to practices and consortium personnel. If they are absent, the system becomes aloof. The system requires both medical and expert management input. Even if staff have a background in NHS management, there is no alternative to GP insight into local services.

## Information technology (IT)

The existing systems of each prospective fundholder should be assessed and a system introduced that answers all their individual needs. However, the same fundholding software must be used by all practices. In practice it is far easier to go for a stand-alone system that allows each practice to keep its existing clinical software. Such a system should, however, allow easy downloading of data from the age/sex register of every practice system.

When choosing software, it is important to establish whether the supplier has considered the needs of consortia. All fundholding systems have been conformance tested against Department of Health specifications. It is therefore the extras that a company offers that become more important. There has been a strong tradition of 'take it or leave it' within GP computing which has left practice IT comparatively underdeveloped, so be careful of the supplier who says 'it can't be done'.

It is important to establish whether the supplier is prepared to consider local needs. The system we now have at Kingston and Richmond Multifund was developed by working closely with Genisyst. The aggregation software that they have developed in response to our needs pools the figures for individual funds. It is not required for fundholding purposes, but is essential if we are to indicate successful management across the consortium and advise funds on the collective effects of their actions.

It is quite feasible to use modems and land-lines to link the individual computers to a central processor. This is only really necessary, however, if the funds are a considerable distance from the central office. If data entry clerks are used, transfer by tape back-up is easier, cheaper, and results in less likelihood of loss or corruption of data. Tape streamers are essential for regular back-ups anyway, particularly if the practice intends to back up both its fundholding and its clinical systems at the same time.

## Funding a multifund

The consortium should be funded purely from the management allowance. This includes staff pay, accommodation costs, office equipment and all subsidiary costs. It is during the crucial preparatory year that balancing the books is most difficult. You will be provided with effectively half the full management allowance, but, if properly executed, the data collection work will require a similar level of data entry activity. Add the set-up costs into this equation and it is obvious why we have argued that the preparatory year allowance is inadequate compared with the allowance for a 'live' year.

The management allowance is not a budget, but is a statement of the upper limit to 100% reimbursement of monies used for fund management purposes. It was originally provided by the Treasury *in addition to* the total NHS budget. Therefore, unused management funds cannot be vired into the main budget and cannot be saved for use in subsequent years. As the role of the consortium develops, it is hoped that the management allowance will find other uses. Full and effective use of the allowance for innovative fund management and strategic planning, for instance, may then be considered as important as making savings.

## Premises

Around 100 square feet per fund is required. More space is desirable, but not necessary. When choosing accommodation, make sure parking provision is adequate and that all costs have been taken into account. These should include rent, business rates, insurance, heating, lighting and maintenance.

## Other costs

Equipment and office furniture form the main bulk of set-up costs. Our own experience is that stationery costs are grossly underestimated.

Finally, from bitter experience, do not skimp on the photocopier. Regular communication with funds and providers is vital and generates the need for large numbers of duplicate letters. A copier that allows the speedy photocopying of several pages per batch with production of collated copies in the original order will quickly pay for itself by saving staff time.

## Types of contract – a consortium viewpoint

To date, smaller numbers of fundholders in a given area have had little overall effect on local providers and have therefore been able to insist on cost-per-case contracts. A large number of fundholders poses a potential problem. A hospital can only base its financial planning on projected income. Where funds go 'cost per case' and commit no money at all in advance, the hospital should theoretically lose staff and close wards to deal with the shortfall. This could then result in the provider finding itself unable to fulfil demands later in the year as the true level of activity is revealed. However, if a fund commits everything 'up front' it loses its flexibility and may find difficulty in dealing with, for example, a sudden increase in the requirement for coronary artery bypass grafts (CABGs) or hip replacements later in the year. In its eagerness to support its local provider it might jeopardize the success of its own fundholding effort.

Until the NHS market system is changed, this dilemma will continue to vex fundholders. Meanwhile, it should be recognized that, although the fund may gain nothing by providing the hospital with some 'readies' in the form of a cost and volume contract, there is nothing to be lost in committing the activity which is already in the system (patients on waiting lists or unnecessarily followed up for years in medical out-patient clinics). This activity 'in the pipeline' might well approach 60–70% of the year's work, since only new or re-referrals will be added during the contracting period. It does the fundholder no harm to include some or all of this in a negotiated deal.

## Agreeing common policies

Practically speaking, there are few areas where GPs need to agree on policies covering more than one fund. Indeed, to do so would be to encourage conformity and stifle individuality. There are simple ways to avoid this.

## Prescribing

It would seem that there should be agreed prescribing guidelines across the funds to avoid disputes. However, a more useful solution, adopted within the multifund, is to employ an independent pharmaceutical adviser. This important member of the consortium team should regularly analyse the PACT data for each fund. Non-threatening, confidential advice can then be given to individual GPs. Our experience is that such advice is heeded and acted upon more readily than FHSA advice.

## Quality

There are benefits to be gained in obtaining consistent quality and pricing standards across all providers. Useful comparisons can then be made between the services offered. At the very least, Patient's Charter guidelines can be insisted upon. Other areas could include:

- waiting times
- discharge slip and discharge letter guidelines
- communications
- faxing of urgent referrals
- drugs on discharge
- staged improvements in services.

## Agreeing prices

The NHS is one of the few markets that insists on purchasers committing money before they know what the provider has to offer. Given that purchasing intentions have to be declared before all the necessary information is available, a major headache has been the habit of providers of 'concealing' part of the cost. (Of course, this concealment is *completely* unintentional – not including capital charges or inflation is a mistake that *anyone* could make!)

It is worth asking the following questions.

- Do all prices received include inflation and capital charges, i.e. is this the actual price each fund will have to pay from 1 April?

- What does the price for each procedure include? To make useful comparisons, it is worth insisting on the price for procedures including *no* follow-up attendances.

- Does the out-patient price include all investigations? If not, what is excluded?

- Is the price an average of several OPCS codes?

Provider price lists come in all shapes and sizes. However, using a spreadsheet such as Microsoft Excel it is quite possible to produce a list of all the major procedures covering all providers.

## Core contract

The core contract should contain quality standards agreed across all funds. To remain flexible to the needs of individual funds the following should be included:

### Provider-specific section

Where a particular provider cannot subscribe to the core contract, it must state in the provider-specific section the areas in which its own provision departs from the core contract.

### Speciality summary

In addition, the contract contains a summary for each specialty. It should include details of waiting times to first out-patient appointment for 'urgent', 'soon' and 'routine' categories. It should also include waiting times for in-patient and day-case operations. Where waiting times differ from those agreed in the core contract, the anomalies should be specified. Some providers might like to use such a section to highlight the special additional services they offer. Others might have special outreach clinics on offer that can be 'advertised' in this section.

## Fund-specific section

Each fund may specify its own individual quality stipulations if it wishes. If the consultation process is successful, this section should be short or absent, since practice needs should be adequately covered by the core contract.

## Monitoring

### Amber Card system

Although working as a consortium offers vast scope for monitoring of services, deviations from agreed standards are more important. Hence the development of the Amber Warning Card system by Roger O'Brien-Hill, chief executive of the Kingston and Richmond Multifund.

Any fundholding GP who is made aware of a specific problem with a provider records basic details of the problem on a simple form. The GP retains a form that includes the patient's details. A carbon copy is sent to multifund headquarters which does not include the patient's details unless the patient consents, but is identifiable by a unique log number. Patient confidentiality is hence preserved. When a sufficient number of complaints about a specific service is produced, this prompts a review, which involves discussions with the hospital and more detailed research.

This method of monitoring can be used by all GPs, whether fundholding or not, but is particularly effective when the results can be pooled.

## Sanctions

It could be argued that it is in the interests of neither provider nor purchaser to be obstructive or difficult in contracting issues, since the two parties are likely to have to meet up again in subsequent years. An element of trust is therefore required on both sides. However, fundholding contracts with NHS providers are merely service agreements. They have no legal basis and neither party can take the other to court if the agreement is broken. (This does not apply to contracts with private providers, which are fully enforceable and should therefore be entered into with great care, and only after obtaining legal advice.)

For this reason, a uniform scheme of sanctions is important. Where consortium funds deal with more than one provider, the record of the individual hospital in meeting contract requirements is quickly broadcast. This in itself serves as a sanction, since funds will become increasingly reluctant to contract with a provider that regularly reneges on agreements.

However, a contract should include a section that allows for a review if a provider is proved to have transgressed consistently. The fund should then have the right to move all or part of the contract to another provider. Where a fund has only one major provider, an agreed staged improvement might be agreed. (It is worth noting that the waiting times published by many providers rank alongside the greatest works of fiction in the English language.)

## Umbrella contracts

It is important to maintain the individuality of the separate funds. Nevertheless, it may well be possible to agree overall levels of activity across the consortium to gain the advantage of marginal costing once a threshold level has been achieved.

## The legal status of practices within consortia and multipractice funds

One of the greatest headaches in setting up the Kingston and Richmond Multifund was the legal status of the individual funds in relation to the consortium and to one another. Equally vexatious was the question of VAT liability. The usual assumption is that any service remotely involving the NHS is VAT exempt. This is not the case, and Customs and Excise, the body that deals with VAT, is a completely different animal from the Inland Revenue.

The difficulty arises because the management allowance can only be used for management purposes (not a great surprise!). By definition, therefore, it cannot be used directly for patient services. The VAT status of the allowance therefore depends upon the use to which it is put. To solve the problem, we turned to a Yorkshire-based organization that advises on the setting-up of workers' co-operatives.

The final structure we adopted and developed was that of the *secondary professional co-operative*. In this system, services and funds are shared, but mutual trading cannot take place if it results in a profit. Should we wish to, we could not, for instance, sell multifund ties, and make an overall profit from one another within the co-operative.

Multipractice funds pose a different problem. At present, from the fundholding point of view, practices in such arrangements are responsible for one another's over-spends. As described below, it is possible to monitor the performance of individual funds, but any agreement that seeks to reduce the liability of one practice for another's over-spend is *illegal* until the rules are changed.

## Monitoring individual practices

Having introduced a system of overall supervision and advice, the monitoring of individual funds is no different from that of a singleton fundholder. The added advantage in the consortium approach is that the performance of individual funds can be compared anonymously. Since the staff making the comparisons are employed by the funds, there is less chance of the advice being seen as part of any potentially threatening policing process.

Reports can be produced for individual funds on at least a monthly basis, showing fund and provider performance. This information can then be anonymized and aggregated using, for example, the software developed by Genisyst specifically for the use of multifunds.

## Dealing with excess use by one or more practices in a multipractice fund

Since the funds have access to immediate independent arbitration in the management team, the risk of serious misuse of the budget is minimized. Although meaningless in law, the portions of the budget corresponding to each practice can be calculated and used as an indicator against which to judge performance. Should a practice be heading for an over-spend of its own nominal portion of the budget, this can be flagged and the reasons sought. Co-operating funds should find less difficulty in accepting responsibility for the over-spend of a partner fund if an independent opinion declares it to be caused by a reasonable use of the budget.

## Use of savings

Any savings can be independently identified and allocated for the use of the individual practice.

# Part 3: The future of fundholding consortia

## Anticipated success

Consortia in the form of multifunds are springing up around the country. They are likely to provide a perfect springboard for the further development of the role of the GP in commissioning. The cautious approval of the BMA for multifunding is welcomed[4], and it is hoped that a similar system adopted universally might also prove acceptable.

# A model for the future

Introducing an extended, universal system of multifunding would allow GPs to be as much or as little involved as they wished in purchasing of all health care and would allow them to enter the scheme with little interference to practice life. Groups of practices covering specific localities would be required to appoint a manager to oversee the day-to-day running of the funds. As long as the patient base were to be over 40 000, fluctuations caused by individual expensive patients would be ironed out and sensible strategic decisions made.

Peripatetic data entry clerks could be introduced so that practices would suffer a minimum of disruption. Health needs would be established at practice level from this accurate information, pooled and used to help formulate a long-term strategy for health care, based on the views of local practices.

The strategic framework for health services in the area could be established in consultation with the existing commissioning bodies and patient representatives. Each consortium would have a statutory responsibility to discuss the overall strategy for the development of health care with all its providers, not just its main local hospital and community unit.

For scarce resources to be used effectively, outcome analysis would have to be carried out and the results acted upon. Public health departments could be developed to assist and advise GPs on local public health policy. The specific data collected for the present health promotion banding could be modified to include specific information for local use.

This system would allow funds to remain individually accountable with health care once again developed locally within an agreed strategic framework.

As this system of practice-based commissioning developed, it might well supersede fundholding. With minor alterations and some semantic juggling, it might also prove acceptable to other political parties.

# References

1   *Health 2000 – The Health and Wealth of the Nation in the 21st Century*. The Labour Party, 1994.

2   Graffy J and Williams J (1994) Purchasing for all: an alternative to fundholding. *British Medical Journal*, **308**: 391–94.

3   Mawhinney B and Nichol D (1993) *Purchasing for Health – A Framework for Action*. NHSME, London, p. 18.

4   BMA declares its support for multifunds. *Fundholding Magazine* (1994), **3(1)**: 6.

# 16 Fundholding and Care Management

## Peter Kemp

The rhetoric of community care is well documented. Health professionals reading *Caring for People*, the local authority source document for the community care reforms, will recognize themes and exhortations from *Working for Patients*. No one will argue with the objective of creating organizational and service frameworks which will enable agencies to collaborate in the delivery of cost-effective services to maintain the independence of older and disabled people. It is, however, too early to say with any certainty whether or not the critical interface at a locality level between care managers and primary health care staff is achieving those objectives in a way which meets the needs of users of the service and their carers. There are, however, several critical features which will need to be addressed if the opportunity to maximize the contribution of community-based services is to be taken.

Care management is the pivot around which a local authority's community care strategy must revolve. Originally entitled 'case management', a term perhaps too closely identified with clinical responsibility for Social Services Departments to feel comfortable in accepting, the concept was broadened to that of care management, which necessarily encompasses systems management as well as individual case responsibility. This generic term reflects not only the local authority's responsibility for undertaking assessments of individual social care needs in collaboration with other professionals but also reinforces the responsibility of care managers to report on aggregations of social, health and housing needs and resource short-falls into the community care planning process. These reponsibilities, combined with the care manager's role in drawing up packages of care to meet individual assessed needs and the widespread development of budget devolution to care management teams, provide a powerful purchasing model in the Social Services Department which has its nearest parallel in fundholding in general practice.

The inherent contradictions in this local purchasing model are clear. One of the major obstacles to effective community care planning between health and social care agencies is the very different perceptions about the driving forces behind the commissioning role. Most Social Services Departments will seek to base their community care plans on perceptions of local needs and service shortfalls. During a planning cycle, purchasing intentions will shift as a result of local information from commissioning teams of care managers on unmet need and resource deficiencies, as well as 'macro'-level planning information, derived largely from standard data sets. A local authority purchasing plan, whilst identifying some areas of volume purchasing, e.g. numbers of nursing and residential beds to be purchased from the independent sector during a particular year, will largely rely on a devolved budgetary system at a local level to enable care management teams to purchase individual care packages based upon assessments of individual need. The emphasis will be upon maximizing choice for the individual, developing imaginative services to maintain the independence of the service user and finding cost-effective alternatives to expensive residential and nursing home placements. By contrast, a District Health Authority (DHA) or Health Commission (HC) will concentrate much more on contracts by volume placed directly with health providers. There will be scant recognition of the need for locally sensitive services nor the assessment of individual health needs and their reflection in the contracting process. Health Trusts rely heavily upon volume contracts to sustain their large-scale businesses and although some HCs are moving towards devolved locality purchasing arrangements, these organizational changes run counter to current NHS Management Executive (NHSME) philosophy. Against this background the GP is the natural ally of the care manager.

At the most basic level, fundholders as purchasers of health-care services will have a clear interest in three areas.

- The criteria which Social Services Departments have developed on which individual assessment and care management decisions are based.

- The principles and objectives agreed between health and social care agencies for purchasing community care services; particularly significant will be assumptions which may have been made about the balance between residential or nursing home care and day and domiciliary services.

- The thresholds set by Social Services Departments which will determine the type and level of provision that the public will be eligible to receive.

Primary health care teams should already have had the opportunity to influence these matters during the first full year of community care implementation and those views should be reflected in the existing protocols and agreements which were required by the Department of Health. However, the agreement of these basic ground-rules at a strategic level must be followed by inter-professional activity at a local level to translate good intentions into improved local services. It does remain the case, however, that much of the potential for collaboration between primary health care teams and care management teams remains unfulfilled. The extension of the hospital and community health services elements of the GP fundholding scheme in April 1993, combined with the inevitable growth of GP fundholding, signals a stronger purchasing foothold for primary health-care teams. The co-terminosity of interests between locally based health and social care purchasers was insufficiently recognized as local authorities struggled to produce their first community care plans. Equally, GPs, fundholding or not, have been notoriously difficult to engage in the strategic planning process and this needs to change if their locality perspective is to make a much-needed contribution to health purchasing plans and joint community care plans. As Health Authorities amalgamate to form larger purchasing organizations, a much stronger local perspective is required if the needs and wishes of patients and their carers for improved health services are to be reflected in health purchasing contracts.

Much of the dialogue about the roles of health and social care agencies in providing better community care services has revolved around things that make collaboration difficult, rather than the issues that unite health- and social-care professionals. Sterile debates around definitions of health care and social care have been replaced by even less helpful distinctions between health gain and social care gain. The concept most likely to unite, not just health- and social-care professionals but those working in the field of housing and environmental health, is that of quality of life gain, which sees the needs of individuals set against the social systems within which they live. The question which professionals must answer is, which 'resource holder' has the expertise, skills and funds to work with others, including the user, to achieve the aims and objectives defined in a 'holistic' care plan? This approach is the most likely to punch holes in inter-professional boundaries, thus achieving a synergy greater than the contributions of individual professionals. Conventional wisdom that such approaches will blur the issue of clinical responsibility, has been undermined over many years by successful, collaborative ventures in enlightened child guidance clinics and in inter-professional teams working with people with learning disabilities and mental health problems. A group of professionals from different backgrounds faced with an inter-disciplinary task, who cannot between them sort out roles, responsi-bilities and contributions to the team effort without invoking manage-ment intervention, will fail to deliver the key objectives of the community care arrangements. If the inter-disciplinary task is clearly focused on 'putting patients first' it will be easier to find ways around inter-disciplinary boundaries.

One of the unifying themes of community care legislation is the focus on needs-led assessments. At the core of the assessment process is the need to focus on causes not symptoms and for that identification of need to shape the resource investments that will be required to achieve positive outcomes for users and carers. In the relationship between pri-mary health care staff and care managers this process is critical, since any potential disputes about case/clinical responsibility are defused as the cause of the problem presented by the patient will define who needs to make the decision with the user and carer about treatment and out-comes. Since a comprehensive assessment depends upon the contribution of professionals in a number of fields, collaborative working between primary health care staff and care managers will facilitate easy access to specialist contributions. In some localities collaborative assessment has developed to the extent that care managers are making initial assess-ments on behalf of other professionals; clearly this can only develop where confidence and trust has been established and where care managers are clearly aware of the limitations of their expertise.

The first and most important care management task is the provision of information for prospective users and carers about the 'needs for which care agencies accept responsibility to offer assistance, and the range of services currently available'. Clearly there are very many ways of achiev-ing this through the many service points available to the public. There is nothing to be gained from providing clear and concise information to users and their carers if, when they make an approach for assistance, there is no capacity to act swiftly and effectively with a minimum of bur-eaucracy. Co-operation between care management teams and GP prac-tices can do much to speed up the rate of response to referrals.

The argument most often articulated by Social Services Departments against the attachment of social workers/care managers to GP practices is that this will draw them into work of a lower priority than would have been the case had they continued to work from within their own agency. Primary health care teams, so the argument goes, would seek to push the responsibility for counselling and support services to the social worker thus freeing them to attend to dedicated health tasks. Current pilot projects in the context of care management report that the major shift is towards early intervention and problem solving, with the patient thus avoiding time-consuming crises which are much more likely to eat into the time of the care manager. Anecdotally, it is reported that a small number of patients take up an inordinate amount of time from health professionals and social care professionals. Very often these patients, who represent a range of social and emotional as well as health needs, are much more likely to be dealt with effectively if they have contact with a single professional who can speak on behalf of the collaborating agencies. This 'holistic' approach based upon an integrated model of care is much more likely to achieve the 'seamless service' envisaged in Department of Health guidance. This integrated model, depending as it does upon collaboration between groups of staff with different professional backgrounds and operating within different managerial and supervisory systems, is most likely to attend to a much neglected role within the care management process. This involves reviewing the progress of the care plan with users and carers and service providers to ensure that services remain relevant to their needs and also to evaluate services as part of the continuing quest for improvement.

It has to be said that whilst this approach to assessment may assist in the process of moving away from service-led to needs-led care plans and that this in turn is more likely to lead, within resource constraints, to a wider choice of creative solutions to meet assessed need, it will present considerable problems to cash-limited GP fundholding practices. Institutional solutions to patient need through hospital, residential or nursing care may remain attractive to hard-pressed GP practices, where needs-led services may call for greater investment from fundholding budgets and where the call on GP time for home visits and emergencies may increase as a result of a greater number of elderly and disabled people remaining in their own homes for longer, with the support of domiciliary and day-care services. Many pilot schemes up and down the country have had the advantage of additional funding for the joint purchasing of services. Would the enthusiasm and creativity evident in many of these pilot schemes have been retained if those joint purchasing initiatives had had to be funded from mainstream social services and fundholding budgets?

The etablishment of good inter-professional relationships is the key to another critical issue: the sharing of information. GPs and care managers who previously worked separately would have dismissed the idea of the sharing of information on patients/clients as counter to the prevailing culture of confidentiality in their individual organizations. It is a sad reflection on the image of Social Services Departments that for many patients their perception of the care manager is substantially enhanced through linkage with a GP practice, and that in this context most of the

pilot schemes report that there is no resistance to the sharing of information within that extended primary care team. Indeed the ease of
access by patients or clients to care managers through the 'one stop shop'
of the GP practice is welcomed by patients, and where other services are
provided on a sessional basis such as 'welfare rights' advice, the patient
avoids a bewildering array of bureaucratic hurdles through which to
assess services. As well as information on individual patients for care
planning purposes, GPs hold an enormous amount of information on a
much wider population than Social Services Departments can ever hope
to come into contact with. There is no evidence that in the past this
information has been used by Family Health Services Authorities
(FHSAs) as part of the community care planning process despite the fact
that such data sets, particularly the material arising out of the screening
process for over-75s, is vital in assisting health and social care agencies
to shift their purchasing priorities.

Much of the impressionistic information gleaned from the attitudes of
GPs towards fundholding suggests an anxiety about their ability to
reconcile the befriending role of the GP with the development of what is
in effect a small business. Can the GP act in the best interests of his or
her patient, advocating the best possible service, in a situation where
ultimately some rationing may need to occur within a cash-limited
budget? That anxiety is understandable and mirrors similar debates
within the voluntary sector about the conflict between the advocacy role
and the provision of contracted services to the local authority. What is
likely to increase the confidence of patients in the GP's ability to
reconcile these tensions is the presence of a range of professionals with
different skills and experiences who can between them, either directly or
by bringing in other services, deal with the needs of the patient as a
whole sensitively, swiftly and effectively.

Not all aspects of the care management role and its link with health-
care professionals will be easy to take on board by GPs. If the wider
primary care team is to be effective in responding to the expressed needs
and wishes of patients, then this commitment may take them into
unfamiliar territory. Research suggests, for instance, that the main pre-
occupation of older people living at home is not the risk of falling or of
admission to residential and nursing care but personal security and safety
within their own homes. How far do primary care teams therefore
provide a brokerage role with the police and with housing agencies to
ensure that as part of a package of care designed to keep an elderly
person in his or her own home proper security is arranged to make this
possible? Again, the provision of suitably adapted housing is essential
if older and disabled people are to continue to live in their familiar

communities. As the inter-professional network around the GP practice increases so it will begin to touch on these wider community systems whose impact in achieving community care objectives may be as powerful as health and social care interventions. The care management role as defined within community care guidance documents has at its core user and carer influence over the provision of health and social care services.

One pilot scheme in the North East has established a locality-based Joint Commissioning Board covering a population of 98 000 which, as well as ensuring that health contracts are sensitized to the needs of the local community, delegates funds to eight locality planning groups in which care managers and health care professionals sit alongside user and carer representatives in determining how their budget will be spent to enhance the existing arrangements. How many GP fundholding practices will tolerate a forum of patients and carers attempting to influence the mix of services to be purchased to meet their needs? The added value of linkage between GP fundholding practices and 'care management teams' is the potential flexibility of the total budget available for health and social care purchasing within that area. Imaginative use of funds would result in the buying in of a range of services to enhance the service and skill mix available to the primary care team in responding to assessed needs. The confidence which will be generated by this process will allow the joint commissioning of services and an increasing use of 'spot purchasing' contracts which will increase the flexibility of the primary care team's response to individual need. Such joint commissioning arrangements will avoid border skirmishes around the differences between a bath performed for social or health reasons or whether domiciliary chiropody is a health or social care service. Given that most people seen by care managers and GPs have health and social care needs which run concurrently, the primary care team may conclude that it does not really matter.

Collaborative work between primary health care teams and care managers will also enable a longer-term assessment of the opportunity costs presented by various treatments. Are combined health and social care purchasing budgets used flexibly more likely to achieve more cost-effective outcomes for patients or clients than if those two agencies continue to spend their resources separately? Can large investment decisions and the outcomes achieved be compared against lower-cost investment decisions and their outcomes, in order to achieve a service mix most likely to optimize resources in the medium to long-term? To that end, the extent to which collaborative arrangements can be enhanced and hitherto separate budgets combined or 'shadowed' the greater the opportunity for assessing the impact of spending decisions on the quality of life of patients and clients.

Whilst many pilot schemes tend to concentrate their efforts on older people over 65 or 75 as major users of health and social care services the potential for this kind of collaboration extends beyond this very narrow definition. GPs will increasingly come into contact with people with learning disabilities and mental health problems who were formerly resident in large institutions. Care managers, many of whom were involved in the assessment and rehabilitation process and who are supporting such people through locality-based services, can contribute enormously to the development of primary care responses to these new and emerging needs.

Equally, Health Authority purchasers must write into contracts the services which provider organizations will have to produce if Health Authorities are to meet their obligations under the Children Act, 1989. It would require a further chapter to amplify the requirements of Section 27 of the Act, which emphasizes the need for joint working between health and social care agencies in identifying children in need and developing appropriate services in response. There can be no doubt, however, that given the continued criticism about the communication between health and social services professionals in relation to child protection, that joint working of the sort described in this chapter can only stimulate a more effective response to children and families in need. The opportunity to move away from reactive reponses to crises in which children are very often the victims towards early intervention through parent education, counselling, support and the development of positive role models must be an outcome worth pursuing.

What is described here may be a vision for the future rather than an appraisal of current realities. Whilst the speed of change and the levels of uncertainty within health and social care organizations may make planning extremely difficult, clients and patients in localities need stable arrangements for access to a range of services. Equally, the aspirations of policy makers at the centre will mean nothing to users and their carers unless there are demonstrable improvements in the quality and range of services. Health and social care alliances at a local level can do much to secure the basic framework of services which most potential users recognize as their natural link into the wider health and social care network.

17  Future Developments

## David Colin-Thome

Writing this piece at the end of April 1994, 3 whole years after the introduction of GP fundholding, the question to be asked is, whither fundholding?

Opponents of fundholding are still as vociferous, even if not as numerous as in the past. What are they opposing? There appear to be two strands to this opposition: emotional and practical.

*Emotional*:
The emotions relate to (a) opponents of any change *per se*, (b) opponents of any change of existing power structures, e.g. hospital units' power and in particular hospital consultants' power, (c) the perceived loss of control. Hospitals in particular and Health Authorities enjoyed unbridled control in the old NHS, whether it be in planning or delivery of services. GP fundholding has challenged appropriately the power barons and control 'freaks' of the centralist, rather bureaucratic NHS. The old NHS seemed to be more about status and process rather than performance and service delivery.

*Practical*:
- Fundholding is too expensive:
  - Computer and management incentives are offered to GP fundholders.
  - Administration on costs relevant to fundholding at Family Health Services Authorities (FHSAs), the old Regional level and the management executive.
  - Clinical time is taken up by administrative tasks.
- Two-tierism. Fundholders are accused of offering better and quicker hospital care for their patients at the expense of non-fundholding GPs' patients.
- Fundholding is too GP orientated and the questions raised are:
  - Are GPs up to this management task?

- Is the GP-dominant model at the expense of other health care professionals?

- Lack of accountability of GP fundholders as managers of NHS resources.

- Achieving savings when the rest of the Health Service is short of money and GP fundholders then further using these savings in ways that may enhance the GP's personal finances.

Despite this mixture of potential problems and issues, and in some cases, tendentious arguments, GP fundholding practices have:

- become better-managed primary care providers, mainly due to the influx of high-quality managers to these practices

- made savings to be spent on primary care developments, thereby facilitating the strategic shift from secondary to primary care

- made savings on budgets which were often set below the budget that they would have received if set on a capitation basis

- demonstrated very little to support the argument of two-tierism and, where this may have occurred, better services could have been purchased for non-fundholding GPs by their often better resourced health authority.

In addition:

- the selection and monitoring of fundholding makes this group of GPs the most accountable of all GPs. The accountability of Health Authorities is often only a paper exercise rather than those Health Authorities demonstrating a visible achievement of quality

- any potential for GPs to make personal gain is severely limited as private companies have been abolished, and any spend of savings has to be approved by the local FHSA.

Many of these issues will have been covered elsewhere in this book, but the issues raised, despite the rebuttal demonstrated by the facts, have to be addressed both by factual arguments and by fundholding developing the scope of the budget and the responsibility and accountability to meet the essentially political nature of the criticisms.

# Extensions

The Secretary of State announced in March 1994 that small practices who feel unable to take on the total responsibility of fundholding can become partial fundholders by choosing from a menu of services they wish to have purchasing responsibility for. This will no doubt encourage GPs who have been nervous about taking on the total responsibility to start in a small, graduated manner. This approach seems to encourage GPs to enjoy the benefits of fundholding without over-burdening them and therefore this approach appears to be an excellent development by the NHS Management Executive for GPs.

The scope for further extensions to the scheme are many and varied, so I will concentrate on the areas that have emerged as key parts of the service which fundholders might purchase.

## Maternity services

Fundholders purchasing community midwifery, hospital antenatal care and possibly maternity in-patient care.

This is an area of responsibility in which many GPs have much practical knowledge and is an area where GP fundholders would feel confident, from the clinical knowledge point of view, in purchasing care. In fact maternity care is an area that GPs have more knowledge of, compared with existing fundholding responsibilities such as purchasing for learning disability and possibly health visiting services.

The problems inherent in this particular extension area are as follows. Community midwives are very assertive, confident, independent practitioners who would in many cases feel that GPs, in being the purchaser, would be one set of professional health workers having too dominant a role over another. Opportunities for conflict are apparent and the example from New Zealand, where independent midwives provide maternity services in competition with the GPs, has produced a more expensive service as the midwives' earnings have soared. The midwives in New Zealand are in attendance with the pregnant woman for much longer than the equivalent GP attendance, and yet their remuneration fees are the same. This has created a situation where the midwives, who also have taken on higher caseloads than was at first suggested, are now not the most cost-effective way of delivering maternity services in New Zealand.

Experience of fundholders in purchasing district nursing and health visitor services has not produced the expected conflict and there have been major attempts to develop the new partnership as witnessed by the March 1994 Joint National Association of Fundholding Practices and Royal College of Nursing Conference. This example of partnership should allay some of the midwives' fears, but there is admittedly an inherent different dimension as maternity care is an area from which GPs, as providers, earn money. The new national maternity initiative, which will enable women to have more choice in their maternity care, may well cause further tension.

I feel maternity services could be included in the fundholding remit, but certainly initially there may need to be some agreed guidelines:

- to allow for any loss of GP earnings

- as for when GP fundholders contract for community nursing services, there should be evidence that fundholders and community trusts should agree quality criteria that both partners should uphold

- of most importance, patient choice and quality care must be sacrosanct. The development of accountability should make such outcomes visible to all, both for GPs as provider and purchaser, and equally for the midwives and their employer.

## Emergency admissions

This is an area which in the winter of 1993–94 became a *cause célèbre* as there was a view that emergency admissions were rising and fundholders were accused of admitting patients as emergencies to avoid paying for their care out of their fundholding budgets. No evidence was found to support these allegations, although in a few areas local variations in emergency admissions rates did emerge, as one might expect. There equally was no evidence that fundholders were succumbing to perverse incentives and admitting patients unnecessarily. There are currently research studies being undertaken to search out more facts to help this discussion. What the furore demonstrated was that emergency admissions could or should come within the fundholding remit. Studies in the USA suggested that to be a health purchaser required a population base of at least 50 000 people to cope with the vagaries of holding a budget. Very expensive cases could totally skew the budget, hence the development of the partial hospital budget in fundholding. Emergency admissions could conceivably make fundholding for a really small population base untenable. There are benefits, however, of holding the budget for emergency admissions. The GP fundholder as a clinical resource manager may, through auditing the emergency referral contacts by hospital medical staff and by other clinical or social care staff in hospital and in the community, alter emergency admission rates. The experience of Castlefields Medical Practice, Runcorn, Cheshire, was that holding a budget gave us the extra incentive to markedly increase audit of the primary–secondary-care interface and reduce referrals across all specialties. Could GP fundholders, by being responsible for emergency admission as part of their fund:

- make more cost-effective use of hospital emergency care, by changing patterns of admission, length of stay and hospital activity costs?

- address the suggestion that they have a perverse incentive to admit?

It is of interest in this area of work that hospital staff are anxious about rates of admission, and yet in most cases seem unable or unwilling to address the issue themselves. If there is a problem of bed shortage or unnecessary admissions *per se*, should not hospital staff be more selective in whom they admit? More experienced admitting doctors could be a more cost-effective utilization of that resource. An issue that in future all purchasers need to address, is their relationships with provider units. Experience seems to suggest that provider units of all types expect more money from purchasers rather than focusing on the provider unit's own inappropriate use of existing resources.

## Accident and Emergency or casualty admission

There are similar concerns expressed about the use of Accident and Emergency services as there are about emergency admissions, and the above text relating to such emergency admissions equally applies to Accident and Emergency department usage. There are, however, some particular issues relevant to this service.

- Following the Royal College of Surgeons' review of services in the 1980s, it was apparent that Accident and Emergency work, to achieve the best results, may well need to be centralized. These central units will depend on speedy transport of emergency patients to such units which contain round-the-clock skilled personnel and up-to-date equipment.

- Casualty (the walking wounded) is a patient service where audit of activity may well reveal alternative models of care:

  – The GP provider should provide more care in his own practice.

- GPs as a more cost-effective model could help staff the hospital casualty service.

- Nurse practitioners could undertake this work more cost effectively.

- Could the hospital make more imaginative use of its casualty department by working with GPs to provide out-of-hours services for the ambulant patient for general practice? This model in the context of the internal market could be a marketing opportunity ensuring GP loyalty to the hospital.

There will be other areas of work that could be added to the scope of fundholding, such as drug dependency work, but such additions would depend on the skills and aptitudes of the primary health care team and these areas may be more relevant to the notion of the purchasing of primary care.


# Total practice budgeting

There are four total practice budget initiatives beginning in April 1994.

- The Worth Valley project in Keighley.
- The West Berkshire project.

Both of these models involve groups of fundholders coming together to manage the non-fundholding element of hospital care. Both schemes will provide indicative budgets for the first year, and the work will be evaluated in conjunction with the NHS Executive.

- The Bromsgrove project is a regional project where four fundholding practices work with a combined population of 39 000 people to manage an actual budget for all their purchasing needs. As GPs' purchasing of non-fundholding elements is ultra vires, the consortium has been given the status of a subcommittee of the Health Authority and is helped by a project manager from the FHSA. This work too is to be independently evaluated.

- The Castlefields project. This is a single-practice project in a practice which is a first-wave fundholder. A practice population of only 12 000 people could leave the practice financially vulnerable if very expensive procedures were necessary for any patient. To address this problem, the practice is to manage directly the fundholding element of its budget and to manage the non-fundholding element for the Health Authority through an indicative budget. Fundholders and Health Authorities, so often in conflict, have in fact complementary skills and different degrees of leverage. Dr S Watkins, Director of Public Health at Stockport Health Authority, describes these differences as bite (fundholders) and leverage (Health Authority). To work together harnessing different skills seems to be the way forward as several opportunities arose from this Castlefields approach.

- The fundholding management allowance has been much criticized as being an unnecessary administrative burden on the health service. With the advent of more professional expertise in the practice as a consequence of the management allowance, not only can the practice be better managed, but also by better contracting leading to a reduction in provider overhead costs, and by devolving purchasing responsibility to the fundholder, reducing Health Authority administrative overheads can demonstrate that the management allowance is a cost-effective use of NHS resources by reducing administrative costs elsewhere in the NHS, as well as developing better primary care.

- Identifying together with the Health Authority wider population needs, not identified easily at the practice population level. Once such need is identified, both purchasers can purchase to meet such needs.

- Working with the health authority so that health authorities and fundholders can meet national NHS objectives, e.g. *Patient's Charter, Caring for People, Health of the Nation*, in a complementary manner.

- Purchasing for clinical effectiveness:

- Clinically orientated contracting. By setting contracts after agreement with the provider clinical staff, for the provider unit to demonstrate a) the development of clinical protocols and b) evidence of audit to ensure protocols and standards are met.

- Work with Directors of Public Health to identify variations in performance and outcomes of various providers' clinical work and contracting only with providers with good outcomes. Such work has been undertaken by Dr Harry Burns, Director of Public Health at Glasgow, who has identified such outcome variations.

- Utilizing the effectiveness bulletins currently being issued by Leeds and York Universities, and by working with the local public health team to challenge clinical practice deemed to be ineffective, e.g. high grommet insertion rates, high tonsillectomy rates, high D and C rates in the under-40s, high hysterectomy rates, inappropriate prescribing, cholesterol screening. The contracting process can be used to ensure that mechanistic approaches to providing medical care can be reduced, unnecessary operations and interventions lessened and the Health Service be more cost effective. Research by Professor David Eddy[1] from the USA, demonstrated that only about 15% of medical activity has ever been scientifically validated. Where no validation or effectiveness has been demonstrated, contracts should be set with provider units where clinical staff are prepared to question and modify much clinical activity.

– Utilizing the same approach to challenge GPs' inappropriate clinical activity, thus enabling monies so released to be spent in response to unmet need.

The Castlefields project is also to be evaluated. Suggested areas of evaluation are:

• change of pattern of referrals, and in particular, emergency admissions, accident and emergency use and maternity services

• total practice budgeting – does this alter or enhance primary care services?

• cost-effectiveness of use of resources, in comparison with the Health Authority use in the rest of the district

• quality of GP care, including activities formerly performed at secondary care level

• clinical effectiveness evaluation at the primary–secondary-care interface

• the changing role of the GP

• effect on reducing or otherwise administrative overheads

• to assess whether clinical criteria are being used in contract setting

• evaluation of whether GP or Health Authority are effective in delivering care in keeping with NHS guidelines

• whether GPs can be engaged in wider community health concerns which are too infrequent to be assessed at practice population level

• the ability to work with a public health focus.

# Primary care-led purchasing

- The GP fundholder needs to be seen as holding a primary care budget. This induces a resource management approach to identify inappropriate resource usage and thus release money to meet need.

- The fundholder, by meeting national objectives such as *Health of the Nation*, will need to redirect revenue to meet such objectives.

- The fundholder needs to use the potential of a registered practice population to identify needs for health and social care. The Castlefields practice has developed such an approach[2]. Needs thus further identified will have to be addressed by setting priorities within available resources. This model suggests that the future GP and primary health care team could be providers of services, purchasers of services and yet also 'micro commissioners' for their practice population. Possessing a budget gives the necessary financial and managerial tools to deliver such an approach.

# Primary care purchasing

The recent reorganization of the NHS means that the local Health Authorities (different forms of merged DHA/FHSA) will be the only statutory authorities in the NHS. Such authorities will need to identify the needs of their population and purchase to meet such needs. The future could herald the purchasing of primary care by Health Authorities to meet such need, a future in which GPs may not be the only provider of services unless the practice can develop this wider role suggested above. The national GP contract may still be the main vehicle to ensure levels of GP provision. A different approach would be a 'national contract' defining national core services, whilst local Health Authorities purchase the rest of primary care from GP practices and others. Such local agreements would depend on locally agreed standards of care being contracted for.

# The future total practice budgetholder

General medical services monies from which GPs' personal incomes derive have not been included in the total practice budget projects. The logical development of a total practice budget is that it should contain all the resources currently available for patient care. Such a development could cause perverse incentives and ethical problems if GPs were allowed to benefit financially from budget under-spends. The solution to such problems could be that:

- GPs are paid a salary set at various levels depending on the range of services and responsibilities the practice wishes to undertake

- GPs are not allowed to utilize under-spends for personal remuneration.

Variants on these may well also emerge.

In the future, however GPs are paid, and whatever range of services and responsibilities GPs are to take on, visible acountability of GPs to the NHS and equally to their patients, needs to be developed. In 1994–95 the Castlefields practice is to offer a corporate contract to its FHSA guaranteeing standards of clinical care, patient access, and of team-work and organization.

Fundholding in its present form has awakened the sleeping giant of general practice. The future development of general practice and of fundholding in particular, can so develop primary care that British general practice will be the rightful pivot of the new NHS and be the envy of all.

# References

1  *British Medical Journal* (1991), **303**: 798–99.

2  Sheaf R, Peel V and Higgins J. (eds.) (1994) *Best Practice in Health Care Commissioning.* Longman, Harlow, Essex.

# Index